The Subversive Vision

. . . art
Is but a vision of reality.

W. B. Yeats, "Ego Dominus Tuus"

KENNIKAT PRESS

NATIONAL UNIVERSITY PUBLICATIONS

SERIES ON LITERARY CRITICISM

General Editor
EUGENE GOODHEART
Professor of Literature, Massachusetts Institute of Technology

MICHAEL J. HOFFMAN

The Subversive Vision

American Romanticism in Literature

National University Publications
KENNIKAT PRESS
Port Washington, N. Y. • London

44114

Library of Congress Catalog Card No. 72-91174
ISBN: 0-8046-9032-4

Manufactured in the United States of America

Published by
Kennikat Press, Inc.
Port Washington, N.Y./London

For Morse Peckham

ACKNOWLEDGMENTS

I wish to thank the editors of *Studies in Romanticism, The Georgia Review,* and *Papers on Language and Literature* for allowing me to publish in revised form essays that originally appeared in their journals.

The manuscript was read in whole or in part by the following colleagues, for whose comments I am grateful: Everett Carter, Marvin Fisher, John Hayden, Peter Hays, Robert Hopkins, Elinore Partridge, Alexander Riasanovsky, and Robert Wiggins.

Two graduate assistants were of great help. Jud Monroe compiled for me a large bibliography of theoretical writings on Romanticism, and Thomas Cousineau translated some difficult French.

The University of Pennsylvania and the University of California, Davis, helped with summer research grants, including three from the latter. In addition, the University of California Research Committee granted me funds for traveling, typing, Xeroxing, and general research. The marvelous secretarial staff of the English department at Davis all had a hand in helping me, particularly Lucille Bonsack, Elaine Bukhari, JoAnn Cedarleaf, Linda Damrell, Betty Kimura, and Jean Walraven. My undergraduate and graduate students deserve thanks for challenging me repeatedly. Almost all the ideas in this book developed out of some connection with classes I have taught.

I want to give special thanks to the following: Robert M. Lumiansky, at whose suggestion I started writing the book in the first place; Dianna Bukey, for moral and emotional support during difficult moments, as well as fine editorial judgment; Robert Merideth, whose comments were crucial in helping me reorganize the original manuscript; James Woodress, for his friendship, loyalty, and understanding of my work; Alex M. Baumgartner, with whom I have discussed American Romanticism endlessly and who is basically responsible for the interpretation of *The Scarlet Letter* that appears in this book; Ruth Hein, whose editing of the copy text was marked by intelligence and discrimination; Diane Hoffman, for her love, her understanding, her enthusiasm, and, most of all, for her belief in me; and finally, Morse Peckham, whose ideas have been the most important part of all my intellectual experience and whose personal example will always be my severest critic.

A book is always a cooperative enterprise. I hope I have not forgotten too many of the people to whom I owe thanks. From those whose names I have mentioned, I beg indulgence for any errors of judgment, taste, and interpretation, for which I alone am responsible.

M. J. H.

CONTENTS

The Subversive Vision

INTRODUCTION

My purpose in writing *The Subversive Vision* is to develop an instrumental theory of American Romanticism. It is surprising how few books have made this attempt, especially considering the immense amount published on this problem in English and European literatures. A serious, sustained examination of American Romanticism as a literary phenomenon has been precluded by the assumption that the United States somehow presents a situation unique in Western experience. Even as fine a book as Matthiessen's *American Renaissance* is guilty of such an assumption. Like any sweeping generalization this one is true enough to be appealing, but it has been used too often as an excuse for ignoring what America has in common with the rest of the world. Cultural chauvinism is not merely a tourist in Bermuda shorts and with a camera; the Ugly American is just as provincial in the academy.

This is not to suggest that there is nothing uniquely American in the circumstances of our country's development. The transplantation of a major culture to an unsettled land did force the emerging society to develop complexities that set it apart from the settled communities of Europe. Certainly the rise of technology in agrarian America was dramatically different in many ways from industrial development in highly urban England. But an examination of major American writings from the time of Poe and Emerson onward soon reveals that their central philosophic and symbolic structures are analogous in most re-

3

spects to what is found, perhaps somewhat earlier, in the major writers of England and Germany. Even given the cultural lag in those days between Europe and the United States, there is a continuity in consciousness on both sides of the Atlantic that recommends a theory of Romantic culture and consciousness that can include all the Western literature of the period.

I have attempted to present such a theory in this book. The experience of cultural upheaval at the end of the eighteenth century was the most important event in Western consciousness since the Protestant Reformation. The whole sense of modern man, his destiny and problems, stems from this time. Once this fact is realized, it is impossible ever again to find satisfactory an approach to American literature that does not take the Romantic breakthrough fully into account. Especially as American literature has become in this century more cosmopolitan and as American culture, fortunately or not, has become the culture of the world, the affinities between our literature and that of other countries must redirect our focus back through the nineteenth century to what led American writers, along with their European contemporaries, to present their readers with the experience and dilemma of Romanticism. Although my detailed analyses are concerned with American writers, my theory includes the experience of Europe; it would not otherwise be valid.

It is because of the breakthrough into Romanticism that our "major" writers — and those in most European literatures since the end of the eighteenth century — have so often been subversive. By this term I refer not to their politics — since many of them were profoundly apolitical — but to their oppositional attitude in philosophy, even occasionally in action, toward the dominant assumptions and institutions of their times. Overlooked in most discussions of American writers is the kernel that today's readers still find relevant and that most disturbed the writers' own contemporaries. For the mark of every major American author since the days of Poe has been an inability to find his culture adequate to his search for value, either in the universe or in his immediate society; and the new ways of looking at the world postulated by these men — different as they were as individuals — were definitely subversive of what has often been called the "official faith," although to each writer the "official faith" meant something different.

In the opening chapter I describe a detailed theory of American Romanticism, based largely on the work of Morse Peckham, at present the leading theoretician in the field. Although his theory is controversial, it is the only one I find comprehensive enough to make sense of both nineteenth- and twentieth-century cultures. Because Peckham is refreshingly unbound by the usual cant about the sanctity of literary experience and because he is not limited by dogmatic political, psychological, and theological preconceptions, he has been able to make sense out of most of the major artists of that time without reducing them to a single one-line tradition. For the trouble with most theories is that they isolate a single strain of thought and push it to absurdity, getting trapped into making their assumptions "logically" continuous whenever these are too narrow to comprehend the material. Finally, Peckham has always been willing to modify his own theory, disagreeing with himself publicly on a number of occasions and in that way exhibiting the mark of a man who has learned from Nietzsche the most important Romantic lesson — that the value of the individual is created by his constant transvaluation of the self and of what the self has been.

Peckham's theory is instrumental. As such, it claims, not to be "true," but rather to be useful in comprehending phenomena. I should like to make the same claim about my own hypotheses. If I turn out to be wrong on certain points, then I expect my claims to be modified, either by myself or by someone else. Writers in the humanities must learn from the scientists to test all their statements in order that they might be disproved. No theory is good enough or comprehensive enough to stand unchanged indefinitely. When theories no longer enable us to see the world properly, they must be discarded like a pair of glasses whose prescription is out of date.

Because a theory is only as good as its application, and as the best way to test the validity of my overall hypothesis, I have chosen to apply my constructs to ten major texts by ten major writers. I have deliberately picked works that, besides being highly representative of their authors — or at least of important stages in their development — have also been the subject of much critical commentary. My readings have convinced me, however, that while my interpretations may in certain particulars coincide with already published opinion, this book's success will depend on how well its theoretical methodology can illuminate a comprehensive body of material. I hope it will be read more as a continuous essay than as a collection of discrete papers.

My only selection which may be questioned as a major work in the career of its author is *Daisy Miller;* but James's contemporaries would not have thought it minor, and I think it sufficiently well known even today to warrant inclusion. I have no elaborate theory about what makes a work or an author "major," although I suspect that the quality of subversiveness may be an element. I picked these particular works to avoid the accusation that I had deliberately stacked the deck in favor of my theory. All the texts discussed are standard in American-literature survey courses, and in that sense at least their inclusion should be beyond argument.

My analytical method is usually a close reading of the text, either in part or in full, with little biographical reference. Nor do I discuss in detail the historical environment in which the works were created. I proceed in this way not because of any New Critical or "contextualist" bias, but because I wish to let the theory speak for itself *in terms of the works themselves,* rather than depending on outside confirmation. If the theory is valid, a more deliberate examination of these works in a historical, biographical, or sociocultural context can also be undertaken. Indeed, such an examination can only strengthen the validity of a legitimate interpretation.

I have also limited myself to writings in prose, since I wish to avoid unnecessary interpretational problems. To shift continuously from prose to poetry would involve using different modes of analysis and might add confusion to an already complex subject. A comparably valid study could be written of a series of nineteenth-century American poems, some even by the same authors I have considered, such as Emerson, Whitman, Thoreau, Poe, Melville, and Crane. But that is the subject of another book.

1

AN INSTRUMENTAL THEORY
OF ROMANTICISM

Romanticism, that maddening word, will never be defined fully enough to cover all cases. At best it can be given a referent specific enough to serve as an intelligible instrument for understanding cultural history and works of literature. The word is generally used in two ways: one, as a timeless quality in art and culture that is contrasted with an entity loosely called Classicism; the other as referring more specifically to a change that seems to have occurred in Western consciousness somewhere around the end of the eighteenth or the beginning of the nineteenth century. I am using the word only in the latter sense. There seems little point in arguing about such matters as whether Shakespeare or Sophocles is either Classic or Romantic; I use the word "Romanticism" to refer, not to a timeless literary quality, but to the innovative culture of the entire nineteenth century, to a new consciousness that made its appearance somewhere around the turn of that century and that bequeathed us problems we have not solved even today. We are in that sense, as others have observed before me, still in a Romantic age.[1]

Before I begin to explain what I mean by Romanticism, I wish to

1. For a compendium of essays theorizing about Romanticism, see Robert Gleckner and Gerald Enscoe, *Romanticism: Points of View* (Englewood Cliffs, N.J.: Prentice-Hall, 1962). The classic essays of Arthur Lovejoy and René Wellek appear here; both of these are to my mind vitiated by trying to define Romanticism through listing its "characteristics" rather than by accounting for it as a change in cultural consciousness. Peckham's early essay, "Toward a Theory of Romanticism," also appears; he has since repudiated most of what it has to say.

state some preliminary cautions. While I realize that categorized descriptions cannot be wholly dispensed with, I am opposed to them. A cultural phenomenon as complex as the Romantic revolution cannot be adequately defined by having applied to it such categories as Medievalism, the return to nature, Byronism, and similar handbook terminology. Nor can Romanticism be effectively characterized by statements that begin, "Romanticism was . . ."; to use the copulative in such a manner is to turn a linguistic concept into a material entity. But even though concepts must be discussed in the same language applied to physical objects, Romanticism never had any such concrete existence. It is a name that has been applied traditionally to a kind of collective cultural consciousness. I wish to locate the beginnings of this shift in cultural consciousness before following its path through a selected body of prose written by Americans and published in the nineteenth century. I do not attempt in any way to present my argument as something that is "true." All historical explanations are only words applied to documents in order to predicate in some not quite clear manner what the past was like. It does no good to demand more of Clio than she can give.

I should like to present in this book an explanatory hypothesis of a body of metaphysical, ethical, and stylistic problems that are a heritage of the nineteenth century. In this effort it is important to isolate as clearly as possible, without reducing them to simple categories, those phenomena of cultural consciousness that remain in some documentary preservation. In addition, the past must remain directly relevant if it is to be worth considering. In that sense I consider myself a self-consciously Romantic historian, like the model presented in Emerson's "History," in that the importance of the past resides for me only in its living relationship to the present moment. Among their many self-appointed tasks, the Romantics had to redefine their own present relationship to the history of their culture. The dialectic of nineteenth-century Romanticism is in large part constituted by the drama of the attempt by all of its major figures to rediscover the individual self's relationship to both his society and the universe. Aside from being a new kind of consciousness, the Romantic orientation is also nothing less than its history. And so, in this book I shall be focusing basically on two aspects: one, the emerging consciousness of Romanticism, and two, the changing shape of this consciousness over the course of a century.[2]

The primary experience that identifies a Romantic is his inevitable consciousness of the void beneath the conventional structures of "reality." It is this initial experience of almost total psychic dislocation, this visceral sense that value and identity have disappeared from the world, that Morse Peckham has called Negative Romanticism. It is both a historical stage in the Romantic dialectic and a necessary step in the psychological development of all men of the Romantic culture. Even figures from the latter parts of the century, such as Melville's Ishmael and Conrad's Marlow, must go through Negative Romantic despair in order to emerge into a further stage of positive self-definition. Young Werther and the Byronic hero are the model Negative Romantics. The stories of Poe are full of characters who have completely ceased to believe in any rationally constituted universe or society and who continually experience the absurd nothingness of the human will. It is not psychically possible, however, to continue for long in such utter disorientation. The leading task, therefore, of the figures after the beginnings of the new culture is to find ways to transcend this state of despair. They have to discover new modes of being-in-the-world, new ways of establishing the self as a repository of value and identity. The Romantic questor must, like Carlyle's Teufelsdroeckh, pass from the Everlasting No through the Center of Indifference to reach the Everlasting Yea.[3]

2. "History is the systematic science of that radical reality, my life. It is therefore a science of the present in the most rigorous and actual sense of the word. Were it not a science of the present, where should we find the past that is commonly assigned to it as theme? The opposite — and customary — interpretation is equivalent to making of the past an abstract, unreal something lying lifeless just where it happened in time, whereas the past is in truth the live, active force that sustains our today. There is no *actio in distans*. The past is not yonder, at the date when it happened, but here, in me. The past is I — by which I mean my life." José Ortega y Gasset, *History as a System and other Essays Toward a Philosophy of History* (New York: Norton, 1961), p. 223.
3. Most of the terminology I use in discussing Romanticism is derived from the theoretical writings of Morse Peckham. Because my ideas are by now so intertwined with his, I shall not document every point of intersection but shall footnote only direct quotations. The major documents from his writing to which I am indebted are "Toward a Theory of Romanticism: II. Reconsiderations," *Studies in Romanticism* I (Autumn 1961), 1–8; *Beyond the Tragic Vision* (New York: Braziller, 1962); the introduction to his anthology, *Romanticism: The Culture of the Nineteenth Century* (New York: Braziller, 1965), which presents the most succinct statement of the theory; and *Victorian Revolutionaries* (New York: Braziller, 1970). Most of Peckham's essays have been collected in *The Triumph of Romanticism* (Columbia: University of South Carolina Press, 1970),

The four most important stages following Negative Romanticism in the nineteenth century that Morse Peckham has distinguished he calls, in order, Analogism, Transcendentalism, Objectism, and Stylism. (I prefer to use the more conventional "Realism" in place of the cumbersome "Objectism.") Because the last of the four does not emerge as an important factor in American literature until the first decade of the present century, it is not a matter of central concern for this book (it is discussed briefly in the conclusion). In European culture the first three of Peckham's stages emerge roughly in chronological order, although in America their sequence is not so neat. This fact can be explained at least in part by cultural lag, a phenomenon certainly not restricted to the United States. It is a complicated problem in writing about American literature that the first three of these stages all become to some extent at least philosophically manifest in the 1830's. Emerson, Poe, and Hawthorne were all at work during that decade, even though most of their best writing was done later. In this book I examine two works from the 1830's: Poe's "Fall of the House of Usher" (1839) and Emerson's *Nature* (1836). While the first is a clear example of Negative Romanticism, Emerson's essay begins as a clear work of Analogism which by the end has moved to a Transcendentalist position that emerged even more strongly in the essays Emerson wrote at the end of the 1830's and the beginning of the 1840's. Hawthorne's "Prophetic Pictures" (1838), by contrast, dramatizes a clear rejection of Emersonian principles through the negatively portrayed artist who resembles the Transcendentalist painter Washington Allston.

A peculiar drama of cultural convergence took place at this time in literary America. Poe was presenting his readers with the earliest variety of Romantic consciousness, that of Negative Romanticism, while Emerson was working out the first of the Positive Romantic solutions, Analogism, in preparation for his more complete Transcendentalist vision. But even as Emerson was busy developing his version of Transcendentalism, Hawthorne was already rejecting it with a world view that I call Realist. All the forces that had by then assumed major cultural importance throughout Europe seemed to burst at once into

---

including the above. I am using the term "being-in-the-world" in the way I understand Heidegger to use it in *Being and Time* and *Introduction to Metaphysics*.

American literature. But even though the temporal unfolding of the various Romantic stages in the United States differs from the European experience, the characteristics common to each stage are remarkably similar in both bodies of literature.[4]

Following his cognition of nothingness, a Romantic figure was first of all faced with discovering a way to project his will upon the external world in order to reassert the dominance of human value and thereby his own identity. Poe attempted to symbolize this assertion of human will through both his psychotic narrators and such superrationalists as Dupin, but because he saw the world as basically meaningless, he was unable to imagine that anything worthwhile could arise from the wills of even extraordinary charismatic men. To mold a meaningless world is still to create nothing. The sense of alienation is both cosmic and social, for in Poe there is almost never a sense that human society has genuine existence, let alone meaning.

In American literature, Emerson was the first to attempt a leap beyond Negative Romanticism. In the earliest part of his career as a writer and lecturer Emerson tried to meet the problem of human valuelessness by constructing an Analogistic symmetry between the individual and the world, self and object. Emerson uses the term "analogist" in his first book, *Nature* (1836). For him man's central task is the need to discover correspondences, to draw analogies between the workings of the mind and the workings of the world. Wordsworth also felt that value was equally inherent in the world and the individual self, and he believed that the individual's achievement of meaning and identity resulted from an intense interaction between subject and object. This vision, by a definite shift in metaphysical assumptions, turns on its head the Enlightenment attitude that is often called nature worship. For the man of Reason, to go into Nature was to search there for the sense of value needed to establish himself as an adapted member of society. Communion with Nature was tantamount to role-rehearsal — witness the quests of Candide and Rasselas.

But for the Analogist such was not the case. Indeed, this stage of Romanticism opposes any kind of role-playing except that of the visionary artist, who through the strength of his "mystical" insights is able to bring about the yoking of subject and object into a single

4. Peckham develops the concept of Positive Romanticism in his early article in *PMLA* LXVI (March 1951). He has since discarded it in favor of his theory of the various stages.

vision of "truth," a Wordsworthian "spot of time." One discovers the
value immanent in the material world that strikes a chord of response
in one's perceptions and cognitions. One thrusts, to use Kant's terminology, beyond phenomena and into noumena to search for the *ding-
an-sich*. This search is essential not only to Analogism, but also to the
whole Romantic tradition. Many of the discernible differences between
the stages of Romanticism lie precisely in the ways their leading
figures attempt to discover the essential "thing" or in how seriously
they consider such a discovery to be possible. Since the search for
this kind of essential factuality is integral to the work of most nineteenth-century writers, the usual claim that the Romantics are un-
interested in fact is to misunderstand their impulses quite badly. For
figures of the Analogic stage the thing-in-itself is discoverable only
through the agency of an almost mystical experience, such as the one,
in *Nature,* in which Emerson describes himself as becoming like a
"transparent eyeball." But while this effort may partially solve the
problem of cosmic alienation, it does nothing to relieve the problem
of meaningful reintegration of the individual with his society.

The difficulties of maintaining this position were understood not
only by Hawthorne and Melville, but also by Emerson, who in trying
to overcome them, moved into the next stage of Romanticism. First of
all, he seems to have asked, if the highest moral experience is a moment
of supreme mystical insight, what can be done with it? The experience
in itself provides neither a guide to action nor a metaphysical ground-
work on which to base a new theory of human value. It is indeed so
pure an experience as to have almost no content. Further, it provides
no way to describe meaningfully the physical nature of reality, since
in such a moment of insight the "real" world becomes only a trans-
parency through which we must look in order to find its nonphysical
value. This circumstance certainly does not solve the problem of
discovering the *ding-an-sich;* it merely elevates a static momentary
insight. And in its elevation of this momentary stasis Analogism denies
not only action but also history, since the latter can play no role in
such a noumenal insight. Finally, and to my mind most fatal, Analogism postulates two sources of human value, and the constant shifting
from subject to object and back — again in a work such as *Nature*
— is evidence of the difficulty of even the greatest writers in trying to
maintain a semblance of coherence in a world where value emanates

equally from more than one source. To see value in both the self and the world is ultimately to see it nowhere, or at least to see the ground of being change too frequently for the meaningful ascription of value anywhere.

Emerson tries to solve the problem by postulating the immanence of value everywhere, not only in the self and the object, but also in a transcendence that stretches beyond and surrounds both. This new vision avoids a symmetrical analogy by positing an asymmetrical theory of value that arises less from a relationship between the self and the world than among the self, the world, and the transcendent value that exists everywhere. In *Romanticism* Peckham suggests that "Transcendentalism deprived the world wholly of value, turned it once again into a meaningless chaos, but preserved the Self and gave the Self's drive for meaning, order, value, and identity a divine authority" (p. 27). I disagree with this contention, for the American Transcendentalists, at least, postulated no such chaos but rather a world that was pervaded indiscriminately with value. Granted that there is in one sense little difference between a world with no value and a world with indiscriminate value, in another sense there is a considerable difference between asserting a meaningless will in a world devoid of meaning, as Poe felt he had to do, and being able, as in Emerson's vision, to draw the source of that will from a mystical cord of transcendence connecting the individual with the spirit that pervades creation. Emerson discovers transcendence everywhere, and he postulates that by drawing on this divine energy, man can both reenter society and activate his redemptive capacity. He expresses this position most fully in *Representative Men* (1850).

It is the Transcendentalist "great man" who is the great nineteenth-century world redeemer, for it is he who draws his redemptive powers and personal value from the vague forces that pervade all of creation, including the individual self. These forces can take the form of Emerson's Oversoul, Marx's Economics, or Hegel's History, but they are always transcendent and permit the rise of the gifted individual who connects himself with the postulated forces and who, in the act of redeeming the world, redeems himself. This cultural energy gives rise to virtuosos, such as Paganini and Liszt, to the theories of Great Men of Carlyle and Emerson, because when the self is connected to universal transcendence it becomes the source of meaning for the world. The "Great Man" creates order through his divine mission. The Enlightenment dichotomy of self and world has finally been turned inside out, for now the individual redeems the world. It is here that Transcendentalism is clearly an advance on Analogism, for it not only makes it possible for the individual to feel a sense of personal identity, it also translates this feeling of identity into a rationale for social action. The individual can at last reenter society.

But Transcendentalism also contained weaknesses, which were ruthlessly pointed out by such writers as Melville and Hawthorne, for although Transcendentalism had finally created a rationale for action by returning the self to a socially active role, it provided no permanent means for making moral decisions. Because the transcending self was its own final moral arbiter, no external limits were imposed on individual actions. Anyone could decide that his authority was drawn from the spiritual transcendence of the universe and could then do pretty much as he pleased. Aside from their antidemocratic and antinomian implications, both of which upset Hawthorne and Melville, Transcendentalist principles provided no legitimate safeguard against the violation of one individual by another. There is, after all, no better way for an individual to establish his identity and power than to make someone else subservient to his will, perhaps even to cause him pain or kill him. And there is nothing in Transcendentalist metaphysics to provide an ethical safeguard against this kind of violation. The misuse of others does violence to the most basic of Romantic emotions, empathy — an emotion that is ironically at the root of all Transcendentalist theories of friendship. The essence of personal morality throughout the nineteenth century lies in the individual's ability to feel with the core of his being what it is like to be another person. To allow a single individual to dominate others without the intervention of any transcendent moral sanction is not only to allow the violation of one human being by another, but to assert the total moral relativity of the human situation.

Hawthorne and Melville saw this basic weakness quite clearly, if somewhat one-sidedly. They were equipped for their insights because each had experienced not only Negative Romantic despair but also a serious flirtation with the seductiveness of Transcendentalism. Although both of them maintain in their works some trappings of the Transcendentalist style, each makes the most astringent criticisms of the previous orientation, breaking with it on the basis of a new vision that has come to be called Realism.

This new stage rejects all mediating visions, it drops as illusory the idea that there is immanent value in either the world or the individual self, and it denies the existence of anything but phenomenal reality. In some respects it believes, like Analogism, that a symmetry must be found between subject and object, with one important difference: all immanent value in either source is denied. The only meaning that can now be found by a character such as Ishmael lies in his direct encounters with the world; not because he might discover meaning either out there or within the self, but because value is discoverable only in the direct confrontation between self and world. Man must know the world as thoroughly as he can, not because this knowledge is intrinsically meaningful, but because in order to survive, man must learn how to live in the world and adapt to its demands. Since all metaphysical systems are therefore illusions, the major human task now becomes the need to overcome all illusion; that is the theme of most Realist literature. One must resist the temptation to believe that illusory "things" — such as society, love, and personality — are anything more than modes of behavior or patterns of adaptation. All former modes of being and perceiving had claimed an absolute value for themselves. But the Realist claims nothing of the kind. For him the only absolute order lies in death. Everything alive is part of the changing phenomena of existence, and as such it can never be fixed into any pattern; any claim to the contrary is just one more illusion.

In the mid-nineteenth century a new alienation springs up that is as profound as that of Negative Romanticism but with the major difference that at least now there is a rationale for the lack of meaning in the world. The world cannot be redeemed; it can only be faced, with unflinching heroism, resignation, and detachment. Aside from being the great age of Realistic fiction, this is also the age of scientific and philosophical positivism; objectivity is the most highly prized human attitude.

It is important at this point to distinguish between the Realist *impulse* that manifests itself in such novels as *Moby-Dick* and *The Scarlet Letter,* novels not normally called Realist, and the Realist *style* that manifests itself in such novels as *Adventures of Huckleberry Finn* and is founded on the philosophical implications of the Realist impulse. Mirroring the attitude on which it is metaphysically based, the Realist style — especially, although not exclusively, in the novel — is primarily designed to be a great instrument of description. Realist writers emphasize detail in their presentation of setting, they attempt to write dialogue that sounds like a literal transcription of speech, they tend to avoid stretching the credibility (or predictability) of fictional events in any way. When speaking in the third person, the Realist narrator is often quite impersonal, either blending his voice into a character's sensibility or standing back from the action "objectively." Verisimilitude is the ultimate goal of the Realistic novelist. When Henry James urges young writers not to "state" but to "render," he presents the goal of the Realist most succinctly. Given the tools of description developed by "Realist" novelists within the literary genre that allows the widest latitude to a descriptivist philosophy of writing (the novel), Emile Zola even believed it could adopt for itself the ends of positivistic science, a goal he carefully works out in his essay "Le Roman Experimental" (1880).

Realism, however, does not remain comfortably within a purely descriptive, nonevaluative metaphysic. Hindsight reveals an apparent necessary evolution from the "Realist" vision to what came to be called "Naturalism." If the only value for man lies in a direct confrontation with purely phenomenal reality, this assumption allows little chance for a positive view of the world. Such a view is, first of all, an illusion — much like a negative view. But there is a difference, for if the individual has what seems to him a continuously negative experience of reality, he will soon come to feel that the world is not merely indifferent toward him, but downright hostile. This is psychologically necessary, for an individual must always see himself as the radiant center of value; and if he is obliged to see the world purely as a set of indifferent, objective phenomena from which he can never draw meaning, and himself as a consciousness that is unable to infuse either the world or his own being with value, then he will soon come to see himself as the victim of hostile circumstance. This view is, at least, more flattering to the ego than the belief that nothing at all makes any difference; it also explains much of the difference in sensibility that appears in novels written at the time — say, in the early works of Mark Twain — and the new sensibility that had overtaken the novel by 1900, when *Sister Carrie* was first published. Dreiser's characters find themselves barely able to deal with the world because they are victimized by a deterministic universe that has robbed them of all choice. Written from within such a deterministic point of view, the Naturalistic novel develops a tone of self-pity that inevitably grows out of a feeling of continuous cosmic violation.

The progression from Realism to Naturalism dramatizes one of the genuine difficulties of the Realist orientation that led ultimately to its decline on the highest artistic levels — in the latter third of the nineteenth century in France and England and in the early 1900's in the United States. A further difficulty is once again the problem of the individual's reentry into society. If the only possibility is either to describe reality or to confront it without a mediating vision, then what imperative exists to act or to join meaningfully in society? (As a sidelight, it seems no accident that during the time the Realist ethic was held most strongly on the upper cultural levels in this country, the American government went through one crisis of corruption after another.[5]) Even if one is to conduct a major encounter with the external world in any of its guises, how can one adequately express or symbolize the value of that encounter when it is not possible to find any meaning at all outside it? It is always necessary to symbolize the value of one thing in terms of something else, but if the encounter itself is the only source of value, then such symbolization is by definition impossible. Finally, as comes clear in an examination of the sentimentality of Theodore Dreiser's Naturalism, the Realist ethic "required a tough-mindedness which even the tough-minded could not endure, for it provided no mode of existence, of getting from day to day" (*Romanticism,* p. 29). If nothing else, mediating visions or orientations, which the Realist ethic ruled out, provide the individual with the only equipment for living that can enable him to endure from one day to the next. It is not possible to live without a strong point of view to structure consciousness. How the inheritors of the Realist ethic dealt with the problems left to them falls just beyond the scope of this book, although I shall suggest in my Conclusion some of the aspects of this "solution."

---

5. "It could probably be shown by facts and figures that there is no distinctly native American criminal class except Congress": Mark Twain, "Pudd'nhead Wilson's New Calendar," in *Following the Equator* (1897).

What follows is a series of detailed and related examinations of ten major prose documents of nineteenth-century American Romanticism. While I have tried to follow a fairly close chronological order in dealing with my choices, my main intention has been to describe the developmental, dialectical progression of American Romanticism both within each stage and from one stage to another. Poe is representative of Negative Romanticism, while Emerson is an Analogist. In addition, the latter explores the beginnings of Transcendentalism by the end of *Nature* and develops them more fully in "The Poet," an essay I discuss in some detail in relation to Whitman. Emerson's colleague and disciple, Henry Thoreau, pushes the implications of Transcendentalist social theory to their conclusion in "Civil Disobedience," and Whitman thrusts the cosmic side of Emerson's metaphysics to its limits in his 1855 Preface. The anti-Transcendentalist reactions of Hawthorne and Melville — measured in the former, violent in the latter — are embodied in the precursive stage of literary realism that I have called the Realist impulse.

The second half of the nineteenth century, following the watershed of the Civil War, saw the full emergence of Realism as both a vision and a style. The major Realists whose work I treat are Twain and James, although I could equally well have dealt with a novel of Howells. Both of the former are ironists, interested in society, although Twain's broader scope and his sustained focus on individual character contrast distinctly with James's concern for manners. I have chosen to deal with Stephen Crane because, although he was a Realist and also something of a Stylist, he is most important as a fledgling Naturalist, particularly in the view of human psychology that controls his portrayal of Henry Fleming. It is just a step from Crane to the ideological determinism of Theodore Dreiser, who in *Sister Carrie* wrote the first genuinely Naturalistic novel in America, and with it closes the nineteenth century for American Romanticism.

2

THE DISCOVERY
OF THE VOID

The House of Usher and Negative Romanticism

Poe is the model Negative Romantic in American literature because it is he who most strongly expresses the sudden sense of emptiness, the perception of the void that lies beneath existence, the despair of finding meaning in the world or fellowship in society — all categories of response that pervade the writings of those who first experience the decline of the Rationalistic world view, an orientation that until then had provided society and the individual with both meaning and value. In Poe's works the Rationalist impulse becomes almost parodic, a tool or plaything of men gone mad. The contrast of madness and rationality was a common eighteenth-century assumption, as Michel Foucault has pointed out in *Madness and Civilization*. In the ways that he contrasts the rational and the insane, Poe unconsciously parodies a major assumption of the previous orientation.[1]

The steady decline of rationalism at the end of the eighteenth century was marked by a dramatic increase in the number of "remissive" outlets for tensions that arose when men discovered that the ways in which they had been used to looking at the world no longer coped

1. Michel Foucault, *Madness and Civilization: a History of Insanity in the Age of Reason,* trans. Richard Howard (New York: Pantheon, 1965). For a fascinating discussion of the nineteenth-century consciousness of the void, see Robert Martin Adams, *Nil: Episodes in the Literary Conquest of Void During the Nineteenth Century* (New York: Oxford, 1966).

adequately with what they were now experiencing. "The Fall of the House of Usher" deals with this historical shift from the late Enlightenment to early Romanticism. While it is dangerous to insist that a writer has a cultural transition *in mind* when writing a tale, I should like to claim that in creating symbolic forms for his stories, Poe expressed a consciousness of the downfall of a whole cultural orientation. That he dramatized this sense of decline in his life as well as in his writings suggests that the appearance in his works of the forms of Negative Romantic despair is an unconscious manifestation of Poe's own sensibility.[2]

In "The Fall of the House of Usher" there are two figures of consequence: a nameless narrator, whose consciousness interprets the events, and Roderick Usher, whose house is the story's setting and whose decline is dramatized in the narrative. Although Usher is usually considered the main character, for me the central figure is finally the narrator, since it is with his consciousness that we are continuously concerned and it is he who is left as the lone survivor, obligated to search for some kind of meaning in the world. Usher is a figure from the old orientation, a symbolic prisoner in his own house, unable even to formulate his own sense of despair, let alone quest for a solution to it. In addition, his obsession with musical instruments, songs, painting, writing, and the almost frenzied creation of pure beauty is most like the remissive obsessions of many late-eighteenth-century figures. It is he who feels his world collapse around him, who cannot integrate into old modes of perception and interpretation the present circumstances that threaten to engulf him.

The narrator describes the day he arrives at the House of Usher as "dull, dark, and soundless," a day distinctly without resonance, in which the clouds hang "oppressively low in the heavens," as he passes "alone, on horseback, through a singularly dreary tract of country" (I, 262).[3] This profound sense of alienation from nature, a consciousness so unlike the wonderfully balanced eighteenth-century ideal, intensifies as the speaker approaches the House of Usher:

2. Philip Rieff develops the concept of "remissive" outlets in *The Triumph of the Therapeutic: Uses of Faith after Freud* (New York: Harper & Row, 1966).
3. Edgar Allan Poe, *The Complete Stories and Poems of Edgar Poe,* ed. Arthur Hobson Quinn and Edward H. O'Neill (New York: Knopf, 1946) I, 262. All page references to this edition appear in the text. "The Fall of the House of Usher" originally appeared in September 1839 in *Burton's Gentleman's Magazine.*

What was it — I paused to think — what was it that so unnerved me in the contemplation of the House of Usher? It was a mystery all insoluble; nor could I grapple with the shadowy fancies that crowded upon me as I pondered. [263]

The world is not only frightening but also pervaded with irrational mystery.

The clue to the nameless narrator's disturbed response is given in "The Haunted Palace," the song Roderick sings in the middle of the story. The poem of that title was published several months before the tale, in *American Museum* of April 1839, and it was almost certainly written before the story. "The Haunted Palace" probably supplied the germ for "The Fall of the House of Usher." It almost perfectly expresses Roderick's dilemma. The poem uses a king and his palace to symbolize the fall of the House of Usher:

> In the greenest of our valleys,
>   By good angels tenanted,
> Once a fair and stately palace —
>   Radiant palace — reared its head.
> In the monarch Thought's dominion —
>   It stood there! [269]

These lines present a time and place in which Thought reigned, a time in which, as in the Enlightenment construct, there was a perfect orientation perceivable by Reason (Thought) between the things of the natural world ("the greenest of our valleys") and those of the mental and spiritual realms ("By good angels tenanted"). King Thought (Reason) reigned in a "radiant palace," a structure aglow with value.

The second stanza informs us that the reign of Reason-Thought is no more. "This — all this — was in the olden/Time long ago" (269). In this vanished time of perfect orientation, the next stanza informs us, spirits moved to "a lute's well-tuned *law*" (italics added). But something mysterious arises to destroy the perfect kingdom of Thought. "Evil things, in robes of sorrow,/Assailed the monarch's high estate" (270). The "evil things" are undefined, just as the decline of Rationalism was often a mystery to the late Enlightenment and Negative Romantic figures, and the old "glory" of the previous age is now "but a dim-remembered story/Of the old time entombed."

The poem concludes with a scene of profound disharmony:

> And travellers now within that valley,
>   Through the red-litten windows see
> Vast forms that move fantastically
>   To a discordant melody;

The formerly "well-tuned law" of the lute is now a "discordant melody." Instead of the clarity of empirical and rational structures, indistinct forms move "fantastically;" the once "radiant" palace glows infernally,

> While, like a rapid ghastly river,
>   Through the pale door;
> A hideous throng rush out forever,
>   And laugh — but smile no more. [270]

The "hideous" throng rushes out of the palace of Thought laughing distractedly, without the smile that connotes well-adjusted humor. Thought's (Reason's) empire has been thoroughly disrupted, and travelers within its valley no longer see anything but irrationality.

In this poem Poe has given the necessary clues for interpreting his story. E. A. Robinson has pointed out that the destruction of the palace of Thought has its correspondence in the destruction of Roderick Usher's rationality. I supplement this contention with my interpretation of the poem, in which the palace of Thought also represents the fall of Enlightenment orientation. Although stories are about people and not about abstract concepts, their symbolic structures often embody better than do the bare statements of an idea a state of mind, an attitude, or an orientation current in the consciousness of a time. In almost all of Poe's "horror" stories we find a counterbalancing of extreme rationalistic logic with irrationality, and more often than not the extremely logical proceeds from the mouths of irrational madmen who people the tales. Reason is often a mere shield behind which madness can hide, and seldom, except in the almost playful tales of ratiocination, does Poe ever view the highly rational with anything but mistrust. As suggested earlier, it is in his parody of the rational that Poe dramatizes the dilemma of the Negative Romantic.[4]

---

4. E. Arthur Robinson, "Order and Sentience in 'The Fall of the House of Usher,'" *PMLA* LXXVI (March 1961), 68–81. Poe's mistrust of the rational intellect is also evident in the first paragraph of "Eleanora," in which he states, "the question is not yet settled, whether madness is or is not the loftiest intelligence."

It is now possible to see the source of the narrator's strange re-actions to the House of Usher. If the house represents in some way the structure of a previous set of cultural values best embodied by its eponymous inhabitant, then the narrator is uneasy in the face of ominously felt, though unseen, signs that both Usher and the structure of his house will collapse; it is a foreboding he cannot understand until much later. He is in this way analogous to the "travellers now within that valley" of the poem. His statement that "the stem of the Usher race, all time-honored as it was, had put forth, at no period, any en-during branch" (264) describes the sterility of those inhabitants of the house who have not given rise to anything lasting; indeed, the family seems inevitably marked for destruction. The speaker's aliena-tion from whatever the House of Usher represents is doubly intensified when he reports that he felt himself in

> an atmosphere which had no affinity with the air of heaven, but which had reeked up from the decayed trees, and the gray wall, and the silent tarn — a pestilent and mystic vapor, dull, sluggish, faintly discernible, and leaden-hued. [264]

There is no longer any unity among the various realms of the external world; there is only decay and pestilence, gray and leaden-hued colors, dullness and sluggishness. Within such an environment man must obviously feel alienated. In such a place reason cannot flourish.

The following description of the house demonstrates even more strongly what the speaker finds wrong with the situation:

> No portion of the masonry had fallen; and there appeared to be a wild inconsistency between its still perfect adaptation of parts, and the crumbling condition of the individual stones. [264]

Though the house is crumbling slowly, it gives no outward sign of dilapidation. The form, still perfect in appearance, is rotten from its core; it is dissolving at all points simultaneously. These suggestions are obvious, but there is more:

> Perhaps the eye of a scrutinizing observer might have discovered a barely perceptible fissure, which, extending from the roof of the building in front, made its way down the wall in a zig-zag direction, until it became lost in the sullen waters of the tarn. [265]

The building has an unapparent, although basic, structural flaw, and one must be a "scrutinizing observer," such as the narrator, in order to see it. If the House of Usher functions metaphorically for the faltering Enlightenment orientation, the symbolism is clear. Our speaker confronts a building that is dissolving all at once and is structurally flawed, even though by outward appearances it is deceptively whole. Its end is imminent. That the jagged fissure becomes "lost in the sullen waters of the tarn" prefigures the collapse of the house into the murky waters that swallow up and hold the secret mysteries of life. But water is not yet wedded to meditation, as it is to become for Ishmael, and its unfathomable mysteries give rise only to that "grim phantasm, FEAR."

The narrator is led through the house by a valet who conducts him "through many dark and intricate passages." On the way the speaker notes many traditional Gothic trappings on the walls, including tapestries and "armorial trophies," to which, as he says, he has "been accustomed from . . . infancy." What strikes him, however, is not a comfortable sense of familiarity, but rather "how unfamiliar were the fancies which ordinary images were stirring up." The dark and intricate passageways — the antithesis of the high Enlightenment ideal of light and simplicity, although increasingly present in late eighteenth-century fiction — fill the Negative Romantic with uneasiness even in familiar surroundings. Something is quite basically wrong.

This impression is fortified when the speaker meets Roderick Usher amid a scattering of books and musical instruments and in "an air of stern, deep, and irredeemable gloom" (265). The inhabitant of the house, the narrator's friend since boyhood, has changed unimaginably. His complexion is "cadaverous," and his unkempt hair flows wildly about his face. He is in a state of extreme nervous excitement, the speaker notes, as if he were a drunkard or opium user. The bonds of his rationality are loosening in the face of an emotional frenzy that steadily rises and lowers in intensity. Roderick feels his reason about to go, and he explains this condition as a congenital disorder.

If the House of Usher symbolizes this particular decay, then as its final inhabitant Roderick Usher draws his constitutional disorder from the same source as the house. The palace of Thought is crumbling in Roderick Usher, in the house that symbolizes both Roderick and the Enlightenment, and in the society of which both Roderick and his house are symbolic representatives. Even Usher's books and musical instruments, manifestations of comfortable Enlightenment culture, lie in scattered disarray. Usher is a prisoner of the old sociocultural

order, and he cannot escape the deterioration of which he is too much
a part. "He was enchained by certain superstitious impressions in
regard to the dwelling which he tenanted, and whence, for many years,
he had never ventured forth" (267). The "superstitious impressions"
are the Enlightenment assumptions which, as they decline, hold Usher
even more tightly in the death grip he cannot break because they are
too much a part of his very being. Usher dwells in a psychological stage
preceding the narrator's, for although the speaker also feels a mysterious sense of alienation, he is nonetheless able to recognize the disparity between what he perceives and what he expects or is expected
to perceive. But Usher is incapable of this distinction; he can only feel
unlocated psychic disharmony. That "for many years" he has not come
outside indicates that his decline and that of the house will be inexorable.

Usher's sister Madeline then enters and floats almost impalpably
through the room. She is "tenderly beloved" by Usher and has been
"his sole companion for long years, his last and only relative on earth"
(267); but she is wasting away from a mysterious disease, and Roderick tells the speaker that her death will leave him " 'the last of the
ancient race of the Ushers.' "

On the night of the narrator's arrival Madeline declines into her
final illness, and during the days that follow, her name is not mentioned by either Roderick or the speaker as they sit together painting,
reading, and singing. Usher uses all the arts to restructure his life
around the void left by his sister's impending death. But every creative
act seems ultimately to objectify his gloomy moral and emotional state,
from "the wild improvisations of his speaking guitar" (268) to the
"pure abstractions" of his paintings. The narrator perceives "the futil-
ity of all attempt at cheering a mind from which darkness . . . poured
forth . . . in one unceasing radiation of gloom." He then describes an
abstract painting by Usher that perfectly symbolizes the state of consciousness recurring throughout the tale:

> A small picture presented the interior of an immensely long and rectan-
> gular vault or tunnel, with low walls, smooth, white, and without inter-
> ruption or device. Certain accessory points of the design served well to
> convey the idea that this excavation lay at an exceeding depth below the
> surface of the earth. No outlet was observed in any portion of its vast
> extent, and no torch or other artificial source of light was discernible;

yet a flood of intense rays rolled throughout, and bathed the whole in a ghastly and inappropriate splendor. [268]

The tunnel has no outlet. It is underneath the earth, a fact that emphasizes its distance from the world of reality. It is a cul-de-sac brilliantly illuminated by an unseen source, implying that the light itself is an illusion. To have the light (of Reason?) shining on an underground tunnel that has no source of ingress or egress is surely an ironic comment on the ability of that beacon to enlighten any part of the world except that hermetically sealed space. It is in such an inescapable underground tunnel — a solipsistic Bastille — that Roderick Usher finds himself imprisoned. The use of such refuges as tunnels, caves, and towers is a standard part of the early Romantic symbolization of the alienated self in retreat from the hostile and chaotic world.

After examining this painting, the narrator hears another of Usher's wildly impassioned songs, and while listening he "perceived, and for the first time, a full consciousness on the part of Usher of the tottering of his lofty reason upon her throne" (269). The song is "The Haunted Palace," and it is clear from the affect with which Usher sings it that the song is another objectification of the decline of "his lofty reason," his sense of self, and his cultural orientation.

The speaker's observation on "The Haunted Palace" is that it sheds light on Usher's belief in the "sentience of all vegetable things," as well as in the sentience of "the kingdom of inorganization" (270). In other words, Roderick Usher himself believes that the stones of his house have a life and will of their own. The fact that they are crumbling is as significant as Usher's own physical decay, because it is these crumbling, moldy, wet walls that he blames for the "terrible influence which for centuries had moulded the destinies of his family, and which made *him* what I [the narrator] now saw him — what he was" (271). The symbolic walls which hold Roderick Usher prisoner are not only those of his house, but also those of the Enlightenment construct itself, a point of view that has hardened into a straitjacket now crumbling of its own inflexibility. Even before their hardening, the narrow conditions that the walls have imposed on the "house" of Usher led to its present state, for the family has been too much a part of its own house to escape declining with it. The Enlightenment construct of an isomorphic relationship between the order of the mind and that of the world external to it is being carried out with vengeance.

Madeline Usher finally succumbs to her illness, and the narrator aids his host in interring the body in a typical Poe crypt, a place "small, damp, and entirely without means of admission for light" (272). That the narrator intends us to view Madeline as a kind of alter ego to her brother is made evident when he says that "sympathies of a scarcely intelligible nature had always existed between them" (272). Roderick seems to feel that he can avoid being involved in the house's decline by burying his sister, but this is exactly what he cannot do. Madeline is not dead; she is in a catatonic state, a fact of which Usher seems at least subconsciously aware. The combination of his guilt and anxiety begins to render him totally mad.

During the following days the speaker witnesses the growing dissolution of his host's mind. Usher's senses have become morbidly acute, and he enters more and more into badly controlled states of hysteria. Finally, a week after Madeline's burial, on an evening filled with rustling draperies and a "rising tempest," Usher comes distraught to the narrator's room, muttering about having seen something that can only be surmised to be the spectre of his sister. The sense of foreboding is increased by "a faintly luminous and distinctly visible gaseous exhalation which hung about and enshrouded the mansion" (273-74). Light itself has become unnatural. To quiet his disturbed friend, the narrator reads him the "Mad Trist" of Launcelot Canning, a title made up by Poe. This is the final instance of the use of art to objectify both the state of Usher's mind and the general fictional situation. Whenever in the "Mad Trist" a door is creaking and wood is being ripped, a corresponding sound echoes throughout the house. After a series of such occurrences, the tension of both Usher and the narrator is almost unbearable. The sounds continue to come closer until their source can no longer be in doubt. Finally, Usher cries out in the extremity of madness and terror:

> "Oh! whither shall I fly? Will she not be here anon? Is she not hurrying to upbraid me for my haste? Have I not heard her footsteps on the stair? Do I not distinguish that heavy and horrible beating of her heart? . . . *Madman! I tell you that she now stands without the door!*" [276]

The narrator is a "madman" to Usher because he does not feel the imminence of disaster as deeply as Roderick. Usher's world is about to collapse, but the speaker is an outsider to this house and to the implications of its constricting walls.

The wind suddenly blows open the doors, and outside them there stands "the lofty and enshrouded figure of the lady Madeline of Usher." After a moment she falls upon her brother, "and in her violent and now final death-agonies, bore him to the floor a corpse, and a victim to the terrors he had anticipated" (276). They have placed her living in the tomb. Usher has attempted to bury what amounts to a piece of himself in order to avoid the destruction that is inherent in his remaining in a house from which he cannot escape. But such an evasion is impossible; Usher is too much a part of his situation to be able to get away.

The narrator, having witnessed the death of his host, runs out into the night, and in the light of the "blood-red moon" he watches the final disintegration of the House of Usher as the "zig-zag" fissure begins to split apart:

> While I gazed, this fissure rapidly widened — there came a fierce breath of the whirlwind — the entire orb of the satellite burst at once upon my sight — my brain reeled as I saw the mighty walls rushing asunder — there was a long tumultuous shouting sound like the voice of a thousand waters — and the deep and dank tarn at my feet closed sullenly and silently over the fragments of the *"House of Usher."* [277]

The structural flaw of the "palace of Thought" has finally widened beyond repair, and the house itself is carried down by its own internal insufficiencies into the waters of the mountain lake. The Enlightenment orientation and the Enlightenment man are swallowed up together.

Water is one of the conventional Romantic symbols. In *Moby-Dick,* for example, Ishmael tells us that "as every one knows, meditation and water are wedded for ever." And at the end of the book, as the "Pequod" sinks beneath the surface, water is the great indifferent equalizer, after having served throughout as the place of quest: "and the great shroud of the sea rolled on as it rolled five thousand years ago." The sea rolls on, indifferent to the little dramas that men enact on its surface. It is in the same sense that the waters of the mountain lake absorb the House of Usher. But otherwise there is a great difference between the two conclusions. As a product of a later stage of Romanticism, Ishmael is able to survive the painful paradoxes of his life by facing them squarely. Ironically saved by a coffin, he is rescued by another questing ship, this one seeking the lost son of its captain, on which Ishmael will presumably be able to "squeeze hands all around," a democratic ideal he stated earlier.[5]

But Poe's nameless narrator has no such consolation, for he believes in neither the value of the individual self nor in the redemptive possibilities of society. He is left alone in the stormy night, everything familiar in his environment having been swallowed up by the water. There is no place where he can find comfort, no orientation he can use to restructure the chaos in which he at last finds himself. In this sense he is truly the "Negative Romantic," and it remains for other American Romantics, such as Emerson, to rebuild the empty and chaotic world in which the narrator of Poe's tale (and Poe himself) feels so out of place.

Poe has used artistic creation throughout "The Fall of the House of Usher" as a metaphor for various emotional attitudes. It seems fair, then, to interpret his story also as an objectification of a dominant emotional and intellectual situation that arose in his day with the decline of an old world view. The House of Usher, symbolic of the Enlightenment, collapses of its own internal weaknesses, leaving the lonely individual with no source of meaning in the world. Usher, culturally imprisoned by the old orientation, dies without understanding what has been wrong with his situation and without being able to escape the constricting bonds of the Enlightenment construct. The nameless narrator (nameless because he can find no means of self-identification) perceives the disparity between the old ways of structuring the world (Usher's ways) and his own perceptions of reality; but he sees no way out of his dilemma, and he is left a lone individual without a sense of self and with no engagement in the world around him — the new post-Enlightenment man, the "Negative Romantic."

5. The best study of water as symbol is still W. H. Auden's *The Enchaféd Flood* (London: Faber & Faber, 1951). Quotations from *Moby-Dick* are from Chapter One, "Loomings"; Chapter 135, "The Chase — Third Day"; and Chapter 94, "A Squeeze of the Hand."

3

FROM ANALOGISM
TO TRANSCENDENTALISM

The problem attendant on Poe's insights should be clear. Negative Romantic despair is neither a perceptual orientation nor a program for action. It is, indeed, defined by the very absence of either a metaphysic or a mode of behavior. And the resultant despair stems from the fact that the Negative Romantic is plunged into depths of nothingness precisely because he has been sundered from the strong belief in both personal and social value that he had derived from the Enlightenment orientation. The resulting Nihilism renders action and even being impossible, for if one feels both the self and the world to be so without value that their very existence is not worth worrying about, then there is neither an imperative to act nor the need to continue existing. Young Werther kills himself, and the narrator of Poe's "House of Usher" can do nothing more than watch his old friend decline and die. The will of even such a strong character as William Wilson is directed only toward his own destruction.

This perception that the world and the self are both potentially without identity or value is nevertheless a necessary first step in Romantic awareness. Before one could attempt, as the generations following Negative Romanticism did, to create value in the world and for the self, one had first to pass through the desperate stage of discovering that all metaphysical systems have no validity outside the minds that formulate and believe in them. Only then did it become possible to begin searching for a new orientation that had no dependence on anything man had ever believed before. If value was now sundered from both the individual and his world, then the task of the emerging generation was to find ways of rediscovering meaning. The first stage of Positive Romanticism — by which I refer to all the stages following Negative Romanticism — attempted to find value in an analogistic symmetry between the inner and the outer, between subject and object. The classic attempt was made by Ralph Waldo Emerson, whose vision is antithetical to Poe's and who by the end of *Nature* (1836), his often bewildering first book, had reached the Transcendentalist thesis that was, like all other orientations, to give rise to its own set of problems.

Emerson's *Nature* and the Struggle for Symmetry

"Man is an analogist, and studies relations in all objects" (I, 27).[1] Emerson makes this statement early in *Nature,* in the section entitled "Language." His discussion of man as an analogist presupposes a human necessity for finding realtionships and balances among whole sets of supposed opposites: the self and the world, the self and society, the inner and the outer, nature and spirit, to name only a few. This search for symmetry characterizes many writers of the period who inherited the Negative Romantic discovery that rationalistic and theistic certainty had dissolved forever. Poe failed to find a new ground of value because he could no longer acknowledge that anything existed except the diseased will of the individual But such writers as Emerson attempted to reconstitute the eighteenth-century isomorphism of mind and nature into a new entity that grew from quite different assumptions. Philosophically, Emerson was an Analogist before he was a Transcendentalist; in fact, he used the Transcendentalist ontology to rescue Analogism from its contradictions.

Nature is not a humble work. It boldly, almost outrageously, tries to solve all the metaphysical problems Emerson felt he had inherited. Foremost among his aspirations was the reconciliation of idealism and empiricism. He expresses this figuratively in Section III, "Beauty," by stating that "broad noon shall be my England of the senses and the understanding; the night shall be my Germany of mystic philosophy and dreams" (17). Emerson's supposed Platonism is more like Kanti-

---

1. *The Complete Works of Ralph Waldo Emerson,* ed. E. W. Emerson (Boston: Houghton Mifflin, (1904). All page references appear in the text.

anism, which, as he notes in "The Transcendentalist," is what passed at that time for Idealism (I, 339-40). Emerson, like Kant, had to extend the empirical tradition of Locke and contemporary science to its limits to show that there was an area of being beyond materialism that the senses were unable to perceive. *Nature* is his first effort in this direction.[2]

The essay's terminology poses a major problem of interpretation. Emerson wants the reader to have "an original relation to the universe," but he builds his argument with the same categories that would have appeared in a treatise of the previous century: "mind" and "nature," "reason" and "understanding," "imagination" and "fancy." What is deceptive is that Emerson — following Coleridge — has redefined his terms and changed the assumptions underlying them so that, although his arguments often sound like Enlightenment theodicy, he has arrived at them by a very different route.[3]

For Emerson mind and nature remain central concepts, but the old isomorphism is no longer there. Although he tries to balance the two, he does not consider nature as deriving order from divine law or the mind as being so structured that it can be redeemed by its contact with and understanding of the natural world. Because of his theory of symbolism Emerson no longer sees nature as the ultimate terrain on which the mind and the senses play, but rather as the entry to a further realm that he variously calls Spirit, God, Reason, Supreme Being, or Universal Spirit. The mind of man can perceive through its contact with nature the ideal structure that underlies all phenomenal and empirical reality. The width of the gap between traditional Enlightenment assumptions and those of Emerson is made clear by a reading of Addison's essays on natural religion in *The Spectator*.[4]

In order to describe the interaction of mind with nature, Emerson redefines three key terms: Reason, Understanding, and Imagina-

---

2. It is not certain whether Emerson had actually read Kant by 1836 or had merely come upon his ideas at second hand in Coleridge, Carlyle, or Brownson. Most of the frequent references to Kant in the *Journals* before 1836 are just in passing and do not indicate a real grappling with Kant's ideas. It is probable that Emerson did not actually read Kant until later.
3. *Nature* has, in fact, proved more baffling to readers than any other work by Emerson. See Merton M. Sealts, Jr., and Alfred R. Ferguson, eds., *Emerson's 'Nature'* (New York: Dodd, Mead, 1969), for documentation of the mixed critical reception Emerson's first book has received since 1836.
4. See, for example, *Spectator* No. 459, in Donald F. Bond, ed., *The Spectator* (Oxford: Clarendon, 1965), IV, 118–20.

tion. In "Language" he presents quite early what seems a confusing definition of Reason — confusing in that he has not yet defined his theory of Idealism and Spirit:

> Man is conscious of a universal soul within or behind his individual life, wherein, as in a firmament, the natures of Justice, Truth, Love, Freedom, arise and shine. This universal soul he calls Reason: it is not mine, or thine, or his, but we are its; we are its property and men. [27]

He reifies Reason as a "universal soul" to be found both inside and outside man and containing abstract entities. In "Discipline" Emerson clarifies his terminology further by the traditional procedure of defining Reason in connection with the understanding:

> The understanding adds, divides, combines, measures, and finds nutriment and room for its activity in this worthy scene. Meantime, Reason transfers all these lessons into its own world of thought, by perceiving the analogy that marries Matter and Mind. [36]

The understanding is that function of mind that both perceives and analyzes phenomenal reality, but that works wholly in this world, while Reason is capable of perceiving the connection between the material and the ideal.

Reason in this passage is within the mind of man, whereas in the earlier quotation it is both within and without. Emerson customarily expects the reader to recall his earlier definitions and to assume that they still continue. He creates difficulties for the reader by spreading his definitions throughout the essay without developing them in what would today be considered a logical, discursive argument. Emerson does define his terms; his early essays are, in fact, composed largely of a series of definitional epigrams; but he builds his arguments by the weight of accumulated examples and related concepts rather than through a progression of interlocking logical blocks.

It is still unclear, however, how reason can bring about the union of spirit and matter that Emerson claims above. Earlier he has described a kind of ideal union of subject and object:

> I become a transparent eyeball; I am nothing; I see all; the currents of the Universal Being circulate through me; I am part or parcel of God. [10]

This is the condition of mystical union, hitherto reserved for the saintly and the insane, but now possible, through the poet, for all men. When Emerson says much later in the essay that "The imagination may be defined to be the use which the Reason makes of the material world" (52), it comes clear that he believes that the imagination results from the action of Reason in "re-forming" the world. It is an integrating function between mind and nature that can make possible the mystical moments by helping man to transcend the senses. Without this concept of transcendence Emerson could never have resolved his basic dualistic dilemma. This struggle toward transcendence lies beneath the surface of *Nature* and is the real source of tension in the essay.

Where does value truly lie — in the self or in the world? At twenty or thirty points in *Nature* the answer to this question could be given with confidence, but each time it would be a different answer and sometimes two answers within a single paragraph. Tracing these constant shifts throughout the essay, in heavy detail, will make clear just how necessary it was for Emerson to employ the ideas of spirit and mystical union. It is only through his appeal to transcendence that Emerson can by the end assert the primacy of human will, and it is only through the positive assertion of will upon a world of immanent value that he can emerge from the Negative Romantic slough of despond.

In his "Introduction" Emerson assumes that nature fills man with meaning:

> Embosomed for a season in nature, *whose floods of life stream around and through us, and invite us, by the powers they supply, to action proportioned to nature,* why should we grope among the dry bones of the past, or put the living generation into masquerade out of its faded wardrobe? [3; italics added]

Nature redeems human life. In the second paragraph Emerson goes on to assume that nature answers all questions and that we can therefore "trust the perfection of the creation" (3). Within a few pages, however, there emerges the primacy Emerson places on the imagination's power to integrate the parts of the world. "There is a property in the horizon which no man has but he whose eye can integrate all the parts, that is, the poet" (8). If nature still possesses within it the principle of order, it nonetheless needs the poet's integrating imagination to do the ordering.

The progression continues during the following paragraph, in which Emerson suggests that nature has only those values man ascribes to it: "Nature is a setting that fits equally well a comic or a mourning piece" (9). He will emphasize this trait increasingly, although he does not now push it to its logical extreme; in fact, he backtracks a bit and concludes the opening section by emphasizing the interrelatedness of man and the natural world:

> The greatest delight which the fields and woods minister is the suggestion of an occult relation between man and the vegetable. I am not alone and unacknowledged. They nod to me, and I to them. [10]
> Yet it is certain that the power to produce this delight does not reside in nature, but in man, or in a harmony of both. [11]

It is not that Emerson cannot make up his mind; he sincerely wishes to locate value in both realms. As soon as he emphasizes one over the other, he has to right the balance in order to conclude ultimately that value is equally present on both sides of his duality. This is the constant problem of the dualist, that leads him always to search for analogies, such as one that appears about a page later: "Nature, in its ministry to man, is not only the material, but is also the process and the result" (13). How is this to be interpreted? Is nature, because it ministers to man, subservient to him? Or is it that, since nature is material, process, and result, its ministry to man is a form of control over him? It would seem from the lines that follow that man is the entity that profits from nature, that the whole process of life is for his benefit. Yet with the phrase "divine charity" in the last line of the paragraph man is put in the position of one who receives alms from all-powerful nature. Clearly the tensions are not resolved.

In the next section, "Beauty," Emerson introduces the most important figurative concept of the essay (and indeed of his life's thought) — that of the eye as the major organ of sense and of sight as the principal organizing factor in human perception:

> The eye is the best of artists. By the mutual action of its structure and of the laws of light, perspective is produced, which integrates every mass of objects, of what character soever, into a well colored and shaded globe, so that where the particular objects are mean and unaffecting, the landscape which they compose is round and symmetrical. [15]

The key words in this passage are "mutual," "laws," "integrates," "globe," "round," and "symmetrical." They stress four primary ideas: perception requires interaction; laws govern the universe; the basic structure of sight is the circle; symmetry is the condition of nature that the senses must discover. Emerson often seems monosensory. The sounds that move Thoreau, the sense of touch that Whitman celebrates, the anxiety feelings of Hawthorne and Melville are almost nowhere in Emerson, for whom contact with reality depends on the sense of sight and the use of the mind.

In discussing the first aspect of beauty, Emerson emphasizes the sanative properties of nature: "To the body and mind which have been cramped by noxious work or company, nature is medicinal and restores their tone" (16). Here nature's function is redemptive, and yet a page later he states: "What was it that nature would say? Was there no meaning in the live repose of the valley behind the mill, and which Homer or Shakespeare could not re-form for me in words?" (17–18) Here nature needs man to "re-form" it, whereas a page earlier it was a medicine for man's salvation. If this seems a contradiction, the integrative function that Emerson saw as essential to true perception must be remembered. The characteristic of man most necessary for this kind of integration we discover in the second aspect of Beauty: "The high and divine beauty which can be loved without effeminacy, is that which is found in combination with the human will" (19). It is the "human will" that Emerson so often ties to the highest and most creative aspects of human consciousness and that must ultimately dominate nature. But it is a different concept of will than Poe's.

The next aspect of Beauty is the spiritual, and the figure that Emerson uses here to personify nature is the mother:

> Nature stretches out her arms to embrace man, only let his thoughts be of equal greatness. Willingly does she follow his steps with the rose and the violet, and bend her lines of grandeur and grace to the decoration of her darling child. Only let his thoughts be of equal scope, and the frame will suit the picture. A virtuous man is in unison with her works, and makes the central figure of the visible sphere. [21-22]

Nature begins as the all-powerful earth mother who will embrace man only if he allows his thoughts to be as great as hers; but by the end of the passage, man, if he has reached the requisite greatness, assumes centrality in the universe as its highest creation. This roundabout process reveals once again the tensions inherent in Emerson's vision.

The third aspect, nature as the object of the intellect, quickly becomes nature re-formed as a work of art. "The beauty of nature reforms itself in the mind, and not for barren contemplation, but for new creation" (23). The intellect is that part of the mind which, like Reason, discovers connections between spirit and nature. It is reason transformed into imagination, which in turn is a manifestation of human will. The man who perceives the world's spiritual reality reforms what he sees into a work of art that "is an abstract or epitome of the world" (23). "Thus in art does Nature work through the will of a man filled with the beauty of her first works" (24). Nature and man interact, but now it is man and his will that dominate.

This attitude continues in "Language":

> All the facts in natural history taken by themselves, have no value, but are barren, like a single sex. But marry it to human history, and it is full of life. [28]

The natural world means nothing unless it is seen by man and in relation to him. This is like the classic question in physics of whether a falling tree makes any noise if no one is there to hear it. Contemporary phenomenology could easily agree with this basic contention, but it is not a position Emerson maintains throughout the essay.

In his attitude toward language — one way that human history is married to natural history — Emerson is at home with Wordsworth, for instance, who, both in the 1800 "Preface to *Lyrical Ballads*" and in the "Appendix, 1802," claimed that the corruption of language reflects the corruption of the human spirit and that the task of the poet is to redeem man by redeeming the language. Emerson combines this attitude with his theory of sight as the central sense in a unique amalgam:

> But wise men pierce this rotten diction and fasten words again to visible things; so that picturesque language is at once a commanding certificate that he who employs it is a man in alliance with truth and God. The moment our discourse rises above the ground line of familiar facts and is inflamed with passion or exalted by thought, it clothes itself in images. [30-31]

Because language is the poet's instrument of redemption and because sight is the highest of the senses, picturesque language, or the most imagistic language, is the best expression of passionate or exalted thought. The exalted man, the man who expresses himself most imagistically, is the one who can perceive the true spiritual reality that lies behind nature. Emerson finally embodies this concept in his Orphic poet, providing himself at last with the key to unlock his dilemma.

Adding the proper language to genuine understanding and reason results in the following:

> At the call of a noble sentiment, again the woods wave, the pines murmur, the river rolls and shines, and the cattle low upon the mountains, as he saw and heard them in his infancy. And with these forms, the spells of persuasion, the keys of power are put into his hands. [31-32]

Man can now dominate and transform the world, clearing away the corruption he has accumulated since infancy.

In "Discipline" Emerson turns from the man-centered creative force represented by art to a position in which he stresses the need for man to discipline himself in understanding and perceiving nature. "Nature is a discipline of the understanding in intellectual truths" (36). One might now expect him to stress the power that nature has over man, and indeed that is how the section begins. We are told that "Nature's dice are always loaded; that in her heaps and rubbish are concealed sure and useful results" (38–39). Nature's immutable laws give it a subtle control over man; and if nature has hidden secrets that are always logical, man must train himself to perceive them. This certainly has an eighteenth-century ring to it. A few paragraphs later, still in the first part of "Discipline," a great change has taken place in the stature of the physical world. Now "Nature is thoroughly mediate. It is made to serve. It receives the dominion of man as meekly as the ass on which the Saviour rode" (40).

How can such a paradox be explained? Does Emerson mean that the dominance of nature, with which he began, is illusory? Rather, in the beginning, nature dominates because man does not yet understand its workings or its relationship to the underlying ideality. The discipline Emerson proposes will finally give man this understanding by forcing him to use the various levels of his reason. Having gained this eminence, he will then be able to invoke both his own potential spirituality and that of nature. Neither position is fixed, but since progress and action are central to Emerson's philosophy, no position can ever remain fixed for very long.

Part two of "Discipline" states that "Sensible objects conform to the premonitions of Reason and reflect the conscience. All things are moral; and in their boundless changes have an unceasing reference to spiritual nature" (40). It is but a step from that premise to seeing the whole universe as pervaded with Unity, a unity arising from the world's spiritual underpinnings.

> Each creature is only a modification of the other: the likeness in them is more than the difference, and their radical law is one and the same. A rule of one art, or a law of one organization, holds true throughout nature. So intimate is this Unity, that, it is easily seen, it lies under the undermost garment of Nature, and betrays its source in Universal Spirit. [44]

Here are the beginnings of Emerson's Transcendentalism — beginnings that necessarily grow from the need for a solution to the central dilemma of his dialectic. The pole of value has swung back and forth between two sources, but now, with the concept of Unity, Emerson can resolve his contradictions by seeing them as halves of a greater unity of which all things are a part. It is a short step from here to the Oversoul.

This development shows how Emerson has attempted to rationalize the difficulties he encountered in trying to move from a world with neither internal nor external value — Poe's world — into a world where value is restructured back into both the "me" and the "not me." Since he cannot make value reside comfortably in either place, Emerson must develop a larger concept that will preside over and contain both.

He moves from "Discipline" to "Idealism," which enables him to give his own cast to the Idealist controversy that so vexed the eighteenth century. Emerson uses many of Kant's Transcendental categories, especially in later writings, and, like Hegel, he emphasizes spirit as the prime mover behind human and natural history. But he adds to both a mysticism stemming more from the Orient than from Europe, a mysticism that drove him finally to submerge all categories into the great One. If for him idealism finally comes to mean spirit, his intention is always to show the natural world as symbolic of the spiritual.[5]

5. Once again, Emerson's knowledge of Kant was almost certainly at second hand; and since he mentions Hegel in his journals only once before 1836 (Alfred R. Ferguson, ed., *The Journals and Miscellaneous Notebooks of Ralph Waldo Emerson,* Cambridge, Mass.: Harvard University Press, 1965, V, 33), it is more than likely that he had not read him either when he wrote *Nature.*

Emerson begins by assuming that the senses cannot be trusted; but, lest it seem that man can question the very existence of the world, he immediately adds that "Any distrust of the permanence of laws would paralyze the faculties of man" (48). He continues by basing man's existence on the fact that nature is permanent:

> The wheels and springs of man are all set to the hypothesis of the permanence of nature. We are not built like a ship to be tossed, but like a house to stand. [48]

By the end of the second paragraph he has changed his grounds very subtly. Now man has something in him that is "stable," while the impermanence of the world makes it but a "spectacle." Emerson does not here invoke Unity to resolve the ambivalence of his dialectic. He uses the concepts of nature as fixed and nature as fluid to distinguish between two types of men: "The sensual man conforms thoughts to things; the poet conforms things to his thoughts. The one esteems nature as rooted and fast; the other, as fluid, and impresses his being thereon" (52). Even when he seems to contradict himself, Emerson quite self-consciously uses the two categories that seem at odds. It was Keats who suggested that one attribute of genius was the ability to remain "in uncertainties, mysteries, doubts, without any irritable reaching after fact and reason."[6] He was referring to the creative artist, and whether this theory can be applied to an essayist whose matter is philosophical thought is at least arguable. But Emerson thought himself more a poet than a philosopher, and he used the former term with all its Transcendentalist overtones.

The final part of "Idealism" is introduced by the following:

> Finally, religion and ethics, which may be fitly called the practice of ideas, or the introduction of ideas into life, have an analogous effect with all lower culture, in degrading nature and suggesting its dependence on spirit. [57-58]

Emerson equates religion with the "practice of ideas" because it "degrades nature." He states further that religion suggests the dependence of nature on spirit. This close equation of idea, spirit, and religion undergoes a couple of transformations. In the last paragraph of "Idealism":

6. Hyder E. Rollins, ed., *The Letters of John Keats, 1814–1821* (Cambridge, Mass.: Harvard University Press, 1958), p. 193. This is Keats's classic definition of "negative capability."

Idealism sees the world in God. It beholds the whole circle of persons and things, of actions and events, of country and religion, not as painfully accumulated, atom after atom, act after act, in an aged creeping Past, but as one vast picture which God paints on the instant eternity for the contemplation of the soul. [60]

For the idealist the world process is not progressive; for him all the world during the act of being perceived exists within its own context, and its history is part of the present consciousness of the world. Emerson's ideal moment of mystical union, in which he becomes a transparent eyeball, can exist quite easily within such an ontology; nor does the ontology contradict the close connection between religion, idealism, and spirit that he posited earlier. It is therefore something of a shock to read in the opening paragraph of "Spirit" that "It is essential to a true theory of nature and of man, that it should contain somewhat progressive" (61). Not only does Emerson deny what he just implied; he now claims that progressivism is necessary and, by implication, that idealism is not; but in so doing, he seems to deny the link he has so painfully established between the ideal and the spiritual. Emerson is not so simple a Platonist as may have appeared.

That Emerson follows "Idealism" with "Spirit" in his chain of the higher being is not surprising; it is confusing, however, that he opens this section by pointing out the difference between idea and spirit after he has seemed all along to demonstrate their identity. This discrepancy can best be explained by the suggestion that for Emerson idealism was more than merely the denial of the material; it is his attempt to get beyond the logical traps of Berkeley and Hume. The world is more than Berkeley thought, more than just the manifestation of a creator thinking matter into being. The world is suffused with a spirit that goes beyond both ideas and matter as they have been narrowly conceived, and that takes its being from the continuous act of becoming the world. Emerson now adds to his concept of spirit its power to create the world rather than merely to stand behind it as its ultimate being. "Spirit creates," he notes midway through this section, and a few lines later he continues in the same vein:

therefore, that spirit, that is, the Supreme Being, does not build up nature around us, but puts it forth through us, as the life of the tree puts forth new branches and leaves through the pores of the old. [64]

Here spirit is not just a counter in a philosophical argument, but the central force that drives the universe and everything in it. The world, through spirit, is now dominant and creates itself *through* man. At this point Emerson tries to bring the spiritual closer to humanity, but he succeeds only partially:

> The world proceeds from the same spirit as the body of man. It is a remoter and inferior incarnation of God, a projection of God in the unconscious. But it differs from the body in one important respect. It is not, like that, now subjected to the human will. Its serene order is inviolable by us. It is, therefore, to us, the present expositor of the divine mind. *It is a fixed point whereby we may measure our departure.* [64-65; italics added]

Because the world is not subject to the human will, it is stable and therefore inviolable. The final sentence contrasts with an earlier statement: "whilst the world is a spectacle, something in [man] himself is stable" (51). The new position certainly reverses the earlier one. As the attachment of spirit and world increasingly manifests itself, man becomes definitely secondary, and even though Emerson begins by claiming that the world and man have the same spiritual origins, he concludes by making quite clear where the superiority lies. At the end of the paragraph he states that "The poet finds something ridiculous in his delight until he is out of the sight of men" (65). This passage suggests that humanity is out of harmony with the magnificence of the natural world, and — to return to an earlier passage — the incongruent factor seems to be the human will. Emerson talks of the "discord" that "is between man and nature," which is also at variance with his suggestion that man and world proceed from the same spirit.

"Prospects," the final section, adds to the reader's bewilderment by immediately contradicting the central thesis of the conclusion of "Spirit" when it talks of "that wonderful congruity which subsists between man and the world" (68). What has happened to the discord? Even more, after the Orphic poet's first song Emerson sees the following vision of the good prospects of the world triumphing over its lower forces:

> Meantime, in the thick darkness, there are not wanting gleams of a better light, — occasional examples of the action of man upon nature with his entire force, — with reason as well as understanding. [72-73]

This passage certainly celebrates human will, an aspect of man that Emerson had found discordant just a few pages earlier. From this tentative beginning Emerson goes on to a full-scale celebration of will:

> But when a faithful thinker, resolute to detach every object from personal relations and see it in the light of thought, shall, at the same time, kindle science with the fire of the holiest affections, then will God go forth anew into the creation. [74]

If man as thinker, creator, and worker of his will assumes primacy anywhere in Emerson, it is certainly here. It is through acting out his spiritual and intellectual potentiality that, for Emerson, man can redeem the world by projecting God Himself into it. He begins the essay's final paragraph:

> So shall we come to look at the world with new eyes. It shall answer the endless inquiry of the intellect, — What is truth? and of the affections, — What is good? by yielding itself passive to the educated Will. [75]

The referent of "it" in the second line is "the world," and it is the world that must yield itself passively to the "educated Will." Man can potentially remake and control the world. The Orphic poet takes over in the next lines, exhorting man to "Know then that the world exists for you" (76) and to "Build therefore your own world. As fast as you conform your life to the pure idea in your mind, that will unfold its great proportions." The visionary poet, one of the chief Romantic figures, exhorts other men also to become visionary poets; to create their own worlds by exercising their wills upon nature and creating thereby — as he puts it in the final sentence — "the kingdom of man over nature" (77).

What are we to make of such a bewildering series of shifts, and how seriously are we to take the final conclusion that Emerson's Orphic poet draws? The problem arises when the traditional categories of logic are applied to Emerson's argument which is only in the loosest sense discursive. Each section of the essay is for the most part logically self-contained, but the essay as a whole does not build its argument in consecutive logical blocks. As a result, many sections seem to contradict the statement just preceding. It seems to me that Emerson is trying to make the strongest possible case for each category *as he deals with it,* be it "Spirit," "Discipline," or "Idealism." But he does not worry about whether statements he makes a few pages later contradict what he claimed before, because each category is its own case.

As a further complication, Emerson uses the same terminology throughout, and in addition, he uses his terminology progressively. A term he has defined in "Idealism" he will use in "Spirit" without redefining it; he merely assumes the already given definition. This leads the reader to believe that there will also be a continuity in the overall argument. He thus expects that one part will lead logically into another and is upset when this progression is absent. Emerson's statement about consistency in "Self-Reliance" is well known; he never pretended to be either a logician or a professional philosopher. His method works, as does Whitman's, by a series of accretions or accumulations, and the concluding logic often seems to take a leap.

If, however, *Nature* is considered as something other than a logical argument, the outcome will be more fruitful. *Nature* is a series of definitions and attitudes that struggle dialectically with a basic metaphysical problem; the dialectic is, in fact, much more important than the logic that *Nature* pretends to present. The fascination of reading the essay lies in watching Emerson struggle with the seeming contradictions in each position, to conclude by positing a poetic solution that transcends traditional constitutive metaphysics. As one of the central metaphysical statements of its time, *Nature* demonstrates well Peckham's contention that for the Romantic authors metaphysics was something instrumental and not constitutive; for Emerson does not conclude with the kind of implacable logic that would suggest he had found *the* solution to his weighty problem. He concludes rather with two perorations from a mythical Orphic poet that resemble the Orphic sayings of Bronson Alcott. These dithyrambs are meant to symbolize the triumph over nature of the will of the truly creative man, the transcendent visionary artist who has plumbed the spiritual depths of both himself and the universe.[7]

I think we must take Emerson's Orphic poet seriously, for he syncretizes a number of elements that have been presented throughout *Nature*. First, Emerson has continuously tried to show the unity and interaction of spirit, mind, and creativity. The figure who unites these qualities most successfully he has called the "poet."

7. Morse Peckham, "Toward a Theory of Romanticism: II. Reconsiderations," *Studies in Romanticism* I (Autumn 1961), 6–7. The same fundamental theoretical assumption is made in Peckham's *Beyond the Tragic Vision* (New York: Braziller, 1962).

In this instance Emerson would seem to have solved the problem that staggered Poe: how to use the human will to restructure the world; for as Emerson defines him, the poet is the man who has found the key to using the will, not only in identifying himself, but also in redeeming the world. The figure of the poet as one who wills man's place in the universe grows directly out of assumptions whose development Emerson scatters throughout the sections of his essay.

Second, Emerson has presented sight as the highest sense and the picturesque as the highest of styles. The hortatory tone of his Orphic poet is Emerson's attempt to make his writing embody the spiritual energies of creativity. Literal picturesqueness is somewhat lacking because the writing is not so much imagistic as it is abstractly conceptual. But this failing lies more in Emerson's prose than in his conception of the poet. For him, the Orphic style becomes symbolic of the human drive for control and orientation — a drive he expresses through the sense of sight and through the concept of the human will's expressing itself. The development proceeds from perception of the physical to conception of the spiritual and finally to the assertion of human will and control through creativity. Thus the Orphic poet solves the problems of Emerson's dialectic by transcending them. Emerson arrives at this transcendence, not by imposing a category external to his argument, but through using concepts that are central to the entire essay. He achieves symmetry, not through logic, but through means that transcend the logical and make it possible for man to reach the ideal Emerson had stated earlier: becoming a transparent eyeball and being at one with the world in a moment of mystical union.

It has not been my intention to give a full exegesis of everything contained in *Nature*. At the risk of distorting some of Emerson's ideas, I have attempted to explore what appears to be the core problem in any understanding of the essay's confusing shifts in argument. One discovery, however, that is shared by all readers of Emerson — even his critics — is how centrally he has expressed what troubled his contemporaries on either side of the Atlantic. Annoying as Emerson's style often is, it has to be understood as *his* way of symbolizing the central metaphysical and social attempt of his time: restructuring a seemingly fallen universe so that man can inhabit it once again and feel himself at its center.

For Emerson this restructuring was a struggle, most visible in

the very involutions of his style. He was too close to the Negative
Romantic discovery of the void to be able simply and coolly to posit
a new order of reality. But for Thoreau, and even more so for Whitman, the Transcendentalist ontology was already a fairly well-estab-
lished orientation, whose validity they could assume and whose ideas
they could extend. Though the confidence of Thoreau and his calculated public stand against bourgeois society is in marked contrast to
the often tentative tone of his teacher, it must be remembered that in
a very real sense Thoreau stood on the shoulders of both Emerson and
Carlyle, the two most important English-speaking authors of the
emergent Transcendentalist orientation.

Thoreau: The Individual *versus* the Institution

   The central dilemma running throughout Romanticism is the
sundering of self and role. If pre-Romantic man felt that society had
either a divine or a rationalistic foundation and that his own sense of
identity sprang from both this society and from a universal order controlled by a deity or by immutable laws, then he could ultimately feel
no conflict between himself as an individual sentient being and himself
as player of a social role. He had no sense, in other words, of "playing a role."

   Romantic consciousness forced nineteenth-century man to realize
both that he had an inner core of identity independent of the world
outside his consciousness and that playing a social role violated this
inner sense of selfhood. It is the feeling of being violated by an inimical
society that lies at the root of Romantic alienation. And yet, if alienation began as an emotional reaction, it also became something of a role
in itself, played at one time or another by all the major Romantic figures. To be the outcast, the exploited outsider who is violated by an
unsympathetic, impersonal society, was a stance familiar to most major
figures of the nineteenth century. Indeed, alienation is today a necessary rite of passage for anyone who wishes to qualify as a "modern"
individual. But alienation is not a final stage: it is the phase associated
most often with Negative Romanticism. Although all Romantic figures

seem to move at some time in their lives through Negative Romantic isolation and alienation, most figures in English literature after Byron and in American literature after Poe find ways to go beyond this early disillusionment in order to reassert the self and to restructure society.

Of all the classic figures of the "American Renaissance" no one felt so radically alienated as Thoreau. In what is still one of the best studies of his thought Joseph Wood Krutch documents Thoreau's cultivation of an almost doctrinal antipathy to the structures of middle-class life and the government that represented it. But even Krutch did not show the depth of Thoreau's commitment to developing many of the traditional Romantic positions in relation to the individual and society.[1]

Thoreau's commitment to Romanticism may be seen by examining two texts: an excerpt from the section on "Economy" in *Walden* and "Civil Disobedience," his classic essay on militant nonviolence.

When Thoreau went to live at Walden, one of his first actions was to write an essay on Carlyle. Like most figures on the moving edge of the culture, Thoreau was seriously impressed with the writing of the dyspeptic Scot, who early in his career had a more responsive audience in the United States than in England. It was Emerson who first managed to have *Sartor Resartus* published as a book, and any reader of the marvelous Emerson-Carlyle correspondence knows something of Carlyle's impact on America. His influence on writers as diverse as Thoreau, Whitman, and Melville, is as astonishing as it is obvious; especially to the modern reader, for whom Carlyle is out of fashion.[2]

Carlyle's most apparent mark on Thoreau occurs in the section on clothes in "Economy." One of the many memorable elements in *Sartor Resartus* is Teufelsdroeckh's theory of the symbolism of clothing. Carlyle in his mask speaks of man as both the tool-making and the symbol-making animal. As *homo symbolicus,* man is a specifically Romantic creature, because he shows the need to find an indirect way of expressing value. In pre-Romantic days the assertion of identity could be

1. Joseph Wood Krutch, *Henry David Thoreau* (New York: Sloane, 1948).
2. Thoreau's essay "Thomas Carlyle and his Works" was first published in *Graham's Magazine,* March and April 1847 and reprinted in *Miscellanies* (1863). *Sartor Resartus* was published in *Fraser's Magazine* from November 1833 to August 1834; it was published in Boston by James Munroe and Company in 1836 and in London by Saunders and Otley in 1838. The definitive edition of the correspondence is Joseph Slater, ed., *The Correspondence of Emerson and Carlyle* (New York: Columbia University Press, 1964).

made more directly, because one could be sure that it lay in some direct relationship between both man and his society and man and his universe. But since that time God had had the bad manners to disappear, and governments had suddenly come to seem the arbitrary adaptational instruments of a species that had to survive. The indirection of symbolism therefore became an increasingly important means of expressing the present crisis of identity and seeing through the older formulations of individual meaning and value. Clothes do make the man, according to Carlyle, but not in the ways we have always thought, because we clothe ourselves in many more items than trousers and shirts. We wear almost everything, both inside and outside our bodies, as a dress for the self. In his broad comic style Carlyle sees even philosophic systems as a form of clothing, and he suggests that all myth has the same ontology as a woolen suit.[3]

Thoreau shares many of Carlyle's comic and symbolic attitudes, although his style is a world apart from the philosophical clowning of Teufelsdroeckh. With his typical interest in paring all human experience down to necessities, Thoreau begins by reminding the reader that clothing, like all other artifacts of humanity, is another extension of man, developed for reasons of function rather than pleasure.

> Let him who has work to do recollect that the object of clothing is, first, to retain the vital heat, and secondly, in this state of society, to cover nakedness, and he may judge how much of any necessary or important work may be accomplished without adding to his wardrobe. [II, 23][4]

But as a Transcendentalist, Thoreau also knows that, because all the works of man emanate from the "Oversoul," they have a moral and spiritual base that must not be ignored. He turns immediately to making ethical judgments about clothing:

> No man ever stood the lower in my estimation for having a patch in his clothes; yet I am sure that there is greater anxiety, commonly, to have fashionable, or at least clean and unpatched clothes, than to have a sound conscience. [24]

He now begins to show the disproportionate importance assumed by

---

3. I use the term "pre-Romantic" not in its conventional reference either to the early Romantics or to the German *Sturm und Drang* figures but simply to refer to those writers who were active previous to the breakthrough into Negative Romanticism.
4. *The Writings of Henry David Thoreau* (Boston: Houghton Mifflin, 1906). All references appear in the text.

clothing. Tending to make luxuries of his necessities, man forgets about such matters as moral virtues. But without a sound conscience, how can he presume to make moral distinctions? Thoreau associates the conscience with that innermost self that the Romantic always tries to protect from violation. But he was quite aware of how the self is hidden, not only beneath such matters as personality, but also under the agglomeration of social roles that are forced upon all individuals who participate in society. Clothing, he recognizes, is one of the chief ways by which people have symbolized social roles; and it is this kind of superficiality, this courting of the exterior, that Thoreau wishes to attack. He knows that clothes are emblems of social status:

> We know but few men, a great many coats and breeches. Dress a scarecrow in your last shift, you standing shiftless by, who would not soonest salute the scarecrow? [24]

Aside from his pun on "shiftless," Thoreau uses ridicule to point out the extent to which men go in assigning value to what covers their bodies. A scarecrow with the right clothing is more impressive than a naked prince. Social station defines not only alternatives in dress but, as long as the convention is upheld, all behavorial choices. Thoreau pushes his point even farther by posing a mock problem:

> It is an interesting question how far men would retain their relative rank if they were divested of their clothes. Could you, in such a case, tell surely of any company of civilized men which belonged to the most respected class? [24-25]

If class distinctions disappear with nakedness, then conventional roles and prescribed behavior become meaningless for people out of uniform. The image of stripping the self bare to shed society's constrictions appears increasingly throughout the nineteenth century. In the ideal Romantic democracy social distinctions dissolve, so that interpersonal relationships can develop without any external mediation.

Thoreau now shifts his ground in order to present conditions in which new clothing might be desirable. The next paragraph begins: "A man who has at length found something to do will not need to get a new suit to do it in" (25). A man must find his own thing to do, but

> I say, beware of all enterprises that require new clothes, and not rather a new wearer of clothes. If there is not a new man, how can the new clothes be made to fit? [26]

If all of a man's actions are interrelated, he must not wear new clothes until he has in some way become a new man; the changing of clothes should be an outward emblem of an inner transformation.

> Perhaps we should never procure a new suit, however ragged or dirty the old, until we have so conducted, so enterprised or sailed in some way, that we feel like new men in the old, and that to retain it would be like keeping new wine in old bottles. [26]

New wine *should* have new bottles, for new contents demand a fresh container. Thoreau would allow a man nothing that has less than a deep relationship to self. As an extension of social custom, clothing can violate a man's sense of identity as easily as a political institution or a mortgaged house. False clothing, clothing that has nothing to do with who a man is, can destroy him.

This extreme insistence on the organic integrity of the self; this understanding of the symbolism of social roles; this suspicion of whatever is "out there" that can tap a chord of response "in here" in order to violate an individual — these are characteristic marks of Thoreau's definition of what constitutes identity and value. Like the organic creature he professes to be, Thoreau carries through this point of view in writings that deal directly with the relationship of individual and government, the institution that so thoroughly pervades our lives. The continuity of Thoreau's thought is nowhere better demonstrated than in another piece he wrote while still at Walden, the famous "Civil Disobedience."

The widespread influence of this legendary speech is well known. Tolstoy, Gandhi, and Martin Luther King, all found it an extraordinary expression of conscience and individual integrity in the face of an oppressive government. For a Transcendentalist all social structures can become oppressive institutions — even fashion in clothing. An examination of "Civil Disobedience" will reveal its close parallels to Thoreau's later statements in *Walden*. The man of letters and the polemicist are two aspects of the same organic self.

If there is any fundamental truth for Transcendentalism, it is that the ground beneath "reality" is spiritual. As in *Nature,* if all individuals draw their being from the same spiritual source, and if spirit is moral, then the most important actions, the only "real" actions, are moral choices. The individual knows whether he is right or wrong because of his "conscience." Though conscience is usually described as being socially trained (much like Freud's superego), Emerson and Thoreau find it to be rooted in that innate spiritual bond between man and all material creation, and they contend that man knows through intuition the differences between right and wrong moral choices. The difficulties of this position are obvious; but the logical conclusion drawn is that, if all things are moral, and if they must thereby have an immediate, direct relationship to spiritual reality, then man must reject anything at all that has a stench of moral expediency, be it clothing or government.

Thoreau notes almost immediately that "Government is at best but an expedient; but most governments are usually, and all governments are sometimes, inexpedient" (IV, 356). Governments, like all institutions, are established to control behavioral ambiguity by reducing the individual's choices. In order even to live in a complex society, people must delegate much moral authority elsewhere, so that they will not have to spend all their time simply coping with survival. This, at least, is how governments begin. Later events, however, differ; for governments, like all institutions, obey the iron law of self-perpetuation, and survival has no connection with moral choice; it only relates to survival. In fact, moral decisions are often inexpedient to the functioning of any institution. That is why Thoreau begins his speech-essay by quoting the statement, "That government is best which governs least," which he then modifies to "not at all." Governments, like all institutions, are necessarily organs of expedience, and as such they constantly threaten the individual's moral integrity by involving him in their necessary compromises. It is important to understand the Transcendentalist assumptions on the basis of which Thoreau attacks the American government.

Thoreau shows his contempt for men in the mass when he states of the government:

> It has not the vitality and force of a single living man; for a single man can bend it to his will. It is a sort of wooden gun to the people themselves. But it is not the less necessary for this; for the people must have some complicated machinery or other, and hear its din, to satisfy that idea of government which they have. [356-57]

Mass man gives over his soul — his powers of moral decision — to a mob that follows conditioned responses rather than the dictates of universal spirit. It is men in the mass who have perverted the democratic ideal by insisting that they as a "majority" have the right to control the lives and moral choices of everyone else. "Can there not be a government in which majorities do not virtually decide right and wrong, but conscience?" (358) But the question answers itself. How can governments, which need great crowds of people simply to keep their machinery whirling, make decisions of conscience? Only individuals can make moral distinctions; and as soon as two individuals incorporate, the possibility is instantaneously diminished that either one will make a decision consistent with spiritual truth. Furthermore, most individuals like the situation as it stands. Because the need to make choices is existentially frightening, most men spend their lives avoiding such necessities. In this avoidance they find a more than willing ally in their government, which gives men a small illusion of participatory freedom in order to convince them that they control their own destinies, whereas in reality it has stolen their moral sense completely.

The instrument used by the government and all institutions to maintain their power and the status quo is that of the law. By creating the illusion that justice is being served through law, governments can once again manipulate this illusion to control their constituents. Like most Romantic writers, Thoreau scores such deception:

> Law never made men a whit more just; and, by means of their respect for it, even the well-disposed are daily made the agents of injustice. [358]

If law is the instrument of the state, and if the state represents either those with the most power or those in the majority, then it can have no relation to any abstract sense of justice: "The lawyer's truth is not Truth, but consistency or a consistent expedience" (384).

Thoreau goes on, in a vein that prefigures Herbert Marcuse's essay on "Repressive Tolerance,"[5] to note that the individual who simply goes along with the state, without either sponsoring or actively engaging in its injustices, who in the name of order obeys the laws because not to do so would be tantamount to anarchy, is just as guilty as the man who partakes directly in the actions of the government. There is no such thing as an uninvolved man, for moral choice consists in taking positive action. "Even voting *for the right*," Thoreau claims, "is *doing* nothing for it. It is only expressing to men feebly your desire that it should prevail" (363). Voting, even if it means voting on

5. See Robert Paul Woolf, Barrington Moore, Jr., and Herbert Marcuse, *A Critique of Pure Tolerance* (Boston: Beacon, 1965).

the correct side of any issue, still constitutes working within the system. Reform, by which Thoreau means ethical change, can come only from people who assert their moral individuality and who, by doing so, break with established institutional channels.

> Those who, while they disapprove of the character and measures of a government, yield to it their allegiance and support are undoubtedly its most conscientious supporters, and so frequently the most serious obstacles to reform. [366]

The truly moral man must disregard his government whenever necessary; he must even, if necessary, "break the law" in order to allow his life to "be a counter-friction to stop the machine" (368). The important thing is to be on the side of the right and not that of a majority, for "any man more right than his neighbors constitutes a majority of one already" (369).

Like most moral absolutists, Thoreau knew himself to be always on the side of the right. Whether or not this accusation is legitimate, its sources can be understood to lie in Transcendentalist metaphysics; Thoreau dramatizes a moral dilemma that has not yet been solved. Even if he is arrogant in assuming his own rightness, he also shows keen insight in pointing out that men cannot consider themselves moral beings if they give over their consciences to the nearest institution. Thoreau, as an individual who is cognizant of the dangers inherent in representative democracy, is entitled by Transcendentalist assumptions to assert that "Under a government which imprisons any unjustly, the true place for a just man is also a prison" (370). It is a statement that prepares the way for Eugene Debs as well as for contemporary resistance movements.

Thoreau's digressions are as illuminating as his main points about the government, and they are ultimately just as much to the point. He speaks of money as an institution that binds a man to it and that controls his moral integrity as much as any government:

> If there were one who lived wholly without the use of money, the State itself would hesitate to demand it of him. But the rich man — not to make any invidious comparison — is always sold to the institution which makes him rich. Absolutely speaking, the more money, the less virtue. [372]

The echoes of Christian asceticism here are not assertions of Christlike piety. Thoreau sees money not merely as an instrument of the devil; he views money and the love of it as a symptom of the middle-class life that invests its energies, not in moral and spiritual capital, but in material accumulation. And the more a man accumulates, the more he needs the protection of governments, armies, and police. It is not simple perversity, antibourgeois paranoia, or anticapitalist asceticism that make Thoreau take such a stance. There is general agreement about the difficulty of remaining idealistic with an accumulation of property, money, and position. "The best thing a man can do for his culture when he is rich," Thoreau notes ironically, "is to endeavor to carry out those schemes which he entertained when he was poor" (372). It is important to realize once again that he sees money and all its surrounding ramifications as institutions that perpetuate themselves by restricting moral choice.

When Thoreau was put in jail for refusing to pay his poll tax, he learned that force is the ultimate foundation of a government. The government is not necessarily rational, although it does create laws to rationalize its operations. What it must do, however, when a citizen refuses it his money or his allegiance — even though the government is supposed to *represent* that very citizen — is either to coerce him into obeying or punish him for refusing. Thoreau's defense against being jailed is ridicule:

> I could not help being struck with the foolishness of that institution which treated me as if I were mere flesh and blood and bones, to be locked up . . . As they could not reach me, they had resolved to punish my body. [375-76]

> Thus the state never intentionally confronts a man's sense, intellectual or moral, but only his body, his senses. It is not armed with superior wit or honesty, but with superior physical strength. [376]

For Thoreau and the Transcendentalists, a man is more than his body or his sentient being. Because he is basically a creature of spirit, mind, and conscience, the mere detention of his body means nothing. It is a testimony to human superficiality that most people view being placed behind bars as tantamount to being destroyed, whereas it should be no more than an annoyance or perhaps even, as Thoreau takes pains to show, a doorway into a set of new experiences and insights. Thoreau describes his cell as being the cleanest and most freshly painted room in town. The jail was the one place in Concord where verses were composed. Thoreau claims that prison actually afforded him a new perspective on the world. By taking such an attitude, he turns the state's punishment into a positive experience. But could a "good citizen" have done so?

Thoreau manages this moral victory because he identifies himself completely within the context of Transcendentalist individualism. He refuses to be classified as part of a mass citizenry, and he pointedly resigns from any society he has not willingly and consciously joined:

> I am not responsible for the successful working of the machinery of society. I am not the son of the engineer. I perceive that, when an acorn and a chestnut fall side by side, the one does not remain inert to make way for the other, but both obey their own rules, and spring and grow and flourish as best they can, till one, perchance, overshadows and destroys the other. If a plant cannot live according to its nature, it dies; and so a man. [376]

A man must live according to his own organic nature; he must "do his own thing." But he cannot do so if he is concerned with making "the machinery of society" work. A man must protect his own moral integrity by refusing to accept the authority of the state. Then he is free to use the state however he wishes.

> In fact, I quietly declare war with the State, after my fashion, though I will still make what use and get what advantage of her I can, as is usual in such cases. [381]

This is hardly a position that Socrates would have sanctioned, but Thoreau was never so perversely idealistic that he would have let the state take his life.

Nor does Thoreau accept the Kantian ethic whereby the individual determines his actions by whether or not the whole of society ought to act as he does. Thoreau *knows* that the great majority of people are not going to listen to him. As he notes in *Walden*, "I do not say that John or Jonathan will realize all this" (367). He would obviously like to reach John and Jonathan, but he has no illusion that he will, and he feels no obligation to act as though all individuals would suddenly follow him in refusing to pay their taxes or in living at Walden Pond.

In addition, Thoreau does not feel that every position he takes must be timeless and eternal. He has an instrumentalist's attitude toward his insights, a pragmatic position typical of Romantic thought:

This, then is my position *at present*. But one cannot be too much on his guard in such a case, lest his action be biased by obstinacy or an undue regard for the opinions of men. Let him see that he does only what belongs to himself and to the hour. [381; italics added]

Like Emerson, Thoreau cares only that the individual, in whatever he does or whatever position he elaborates, feel a strong sense of the moral rightness of his choice *at that moment* and be responsible only to himself and not to his need to please others. To worry about more than the rightness of the moment, to choose all one's actions with an eye toward history, is to lose the chance to act at all, and for a Transcendentalist action is the only justification of philosophical thought.

Thoreau knows too that neither reform nor any change in point of view comes from within the institution:

Statesmen and legislators, standing so completely within the institution, never distinctly and nakedly behold it. They speak of moving society, but have no resting-place without it. [384]

This ability to be both within and without a situation — to see oneself, so to speak, at right angles — becomes increasingly important in the nineteenth century. It is a situation of which Emerson shows cognizance in his essay "Circles" and an attitude that Whitman dramatizes in "Song of Myself." A man who operates completely within the institution cannot see beyond its governing assumptions. This is a remarkably contemporary insight. In *The Structure of Scientific Revolutions,* Thomas Kuhn uses the development of a number of scientific theories to document the process whereby loyalty to assumptions that have given someone new insights in turn blinds him to the new assumptions needed to break through to further insights. A strong gestalt prevents the individual from seeing contradictions from the outside.[6]

Although Thoreau has not worked out a new form of government, he is practical enough to know that all systems are ultimately subject to the iron law of institutions and vulnerable to expedience; he is, however, utopian enough to want the kind of participatory democracy that allows an individual to do as he likes.

There will never be a really free and enlightened State until the State comes to recognize the individual as a higher and independent power, from which all its own power and authority are derived, and treats him accordingly. [387]

6. Thomas Kuhn, *The Structure of Scientific Revolutions* (Chicago: University of Chicago Press, 1962).

If this thought sounds initially like the American ideal taught in all civics classes, a little longer look makes it seem quite subversive. No government now or ever has allowed its citizens this kind of personal consideration. It would not be a government if it did — at least, not a government as we know it. But maybe that is the author's point.

It is easy to accuse Thoreau of being naive and impractical; that is how utopian visions are always dismissed. How could we continue as a country if men refused to respect our institutions? The country would change tremendously; but short of revolution, the question is moot. To dismiss Thoreau lightly, however, is to overlook the strength of his criticism of our institutions and of the rhetoric that has always given us Americans such a false view of how they really do operate. Most of us identify with our government not as it really is, but as an entity created by propaganda and drummed into our consciousness by years of schooling, listening to political addresses, reading the newspapers, hearing the radio, watching television. Our government does not, and never did, operate in the way described in the civics books. Thoreau constantly points out how all institutions work to violate individuals. It is important to realize the extent to which Thoreau is driven to this stance by the position he occupied in the continuing Romantic dialectic.

Thoreau is a distinctly transitional figure. It is too easy to identify him solely with Transcendentalism. While most of his metaphysical and ethical assumptions arise from the same sources as those of Emerson, he moves beyond his fellow Transcendentalists — for whom he often had little patience — in his efforts to strip down to the bedrock of self. When Thoreau talks about "Economy" in *Walden,* he means it. He wants to see how little we can do with, how much of the institutional gum he can strip away from our eyes (to borrow an image from Whitman) so as to return us to the energies within the individual himself. This attempt to strip away all mediating orientations is quite different from the attempt of Emerson, who wanted to build an elaborate structure through which one could see the world and make the moral choices necessary to a truly spiritual existence. While Thoreau starts from similar assumptions, he quickly drops all the accompanying apparatus and simply assumes the Transcendentalist ontology. What is important is the struggle for selfhood which includes living economically and seeing the world economically — in other words, purely for what it presents to the senses. The difficulties inherent in this effort, however, Thoreau only begins to touch on, although his later journals, with their relative absence of philosophizing and their endless catalogue of naturalistic detail, give evidence of the direction in which Thoreau was moving at the time of his death.

It remains, however, for Hawthorne and Melville to explore for American literature the problems of direct confrontation with an unmediated world. Thoreau worked too much within the body of Transcendentalist assumption ever to break fully with it, although it is impossible to know how far he might have gone had he lived another twenty years. His writing furnishes the strongest example of the Transcendentalist drive to reintegrate the individual with his society, as well as a powerful expression of Transcendentalist individualism and alienation. Walt Whitman is another kind of Transcendentalist activist, although the primary interest in his work is his use of Transcendentalist assumptions to develop a kind of religious mysticism. In Whitman the "imperial self" is almost totally transcendent in its need to find divinity within, an ample corrective to Negative Romantic despair and a logical derivative from Emersonian principles. The next section will discuss Whitman's debt to Emerson preparatory to dealing with the development of the poet's own mystical system in his 1855 Preface to *Leaves of Grass*.[7]

Whitman's Preface: Every Man His Own Priest

It was neither Emerson nor Thoreau, but a New Yorker named Walt Whitman who wrote the most representative Transcendentalist document in American prose — the 1855 Preface to *Leaves of Grass*. Like Thoreau, Whitman did not have to struggle with the problems of an emergent orientation; Transcendentalism was an established attitude, a way of looking at the world he could inherit from his culture, absorbing it not just from the air but also from the program of America's leading man of letters. Drawing on Emerson's authority, Whitman could present his vision without either his mentor's initial doubts or the struggling contradictions of Emerson's dialectic.

7. See Quentin Anderson, *The Imperial Self: An Essay in American Literary and Cultural History* (New York: Knopf, 1971).

Emerson's letter to thank Whitman for his gift copy of *Leaves* is too well known for further comment. Emerson no doubt recognized that the prescription he had written in "The Poet" (1844) was now fulfilled. A look at the essay shows just how much of Emerson's thought Whitman appropriated. Without suggesting that Whitman is unoriginal, it seems clear that after reading "The Poet," he felt something akin to a "call."

The poet is one of the "representative men." *Nature* demonstrates that for Emerson the divinity that is inherent everywhere manifests itself by the agency of a representative individual who embodies spiritual truth. In "The Poet" he elaborates on this idea:

> The poet . . . is the man without impediment, who sees and handles that which others dream of, traverses the whole scale of experience, and is representative of man, in virtue of being the largest power to receive and to impart. [III, 6][1]

More than being just a writer of verse, the poet is in touch with cosmic realities and sensitive to the universal heartbeat.

Emerson notes that "the Universe has three children, . . . the Knower, the Doer and the Sayer," who are models for humanity. He describes these roles in terms of their characteristic action and defines all actions as emanating from divine energy. "Words are also actions, and actions are a kind of words" (8). In that sense writing a poem is equivalent to leading an army, going into nature, or governing a people. The poet, as distinguished from the mere versifier, has all of history in his consciousness because all true poems are contained within the character of the universe long before anyone translates them into words. The poet is therefore by his actions a prophet and, since all things not only have meaning but are related to everything else through the thread of spirit, symbolism is the basic language of poetry. "Things admit of being used as symbols because nature is a symbol, in the whole, and in every part" (13). The dialectic of *Nature* underlies all the statements Emerson makes in his *Essays*.

His theory of prosody, which directly prefigures Whitman's, is an outgrowth of Transcendentalist organicism:

1. *The Complete Works of Ralph Waldo Emerson,* ed. and introd. E. W. Emerson (Boston: Houghton Mifflin, 1904). All references appear in the text.

> For it is not metres, but a metre-making argument that makes a
> poem, — a thought so passionate and alive that like the spirit of a plant
> or an animal it has an architecture of its own, and adorns nature with a
> new thing. The thought and the form are equal in the order of time, but
> in the order of genesis the thought is prior to the form. [9-10]

Any external system, even a preconceived poetic form, is an imposition
on nature. Inherent in all matter are its organic forms, and if one seeks
the noumenal reality of one's subject, its organic form will always
emerge. The poet "uses forms according to the life, and not according
to the form" (21). By "the life" in forms Emerson has in mind the
same phenomenon Wordsworth called the divine "breath."[2]

In order to uncover this "life," one must wash away all illusion
and seek beneath the surface for "the true nectar, which is the ravish-
ment of the intellect by coming nearer to the fact" (28). The fact *is*
the truth and the poet is the man who can discover facts beneath sur-
faces, making us "like persons who come out of a cave or cellar into
the open air" (30). This allusion to Plato's cave is similar to Whitman's image in *Song of Myself:*

> Long enough have you dreamed contemptible dreams,
> Now I wash the gum from your eyes,
>   You must habit yourself to the dazzle of the light and of every
> moment of your life. [81][3]

The redemptive poet blinds humanity with the truth. "The poets are
thus liberating gods," states Emerson. "They are free, and they make
free" (32). However, he adds, "I look in vain for the poet whom I
describe" (37).

In order to find the poet he describes, Emerson writes a prescription for him, exhorting the emerging bard to mold his poetry from
American materials. This poet will create our mythology by singing
our past and prophesying our future. In a short catalogue, prefiguring

---

2.   For I, methought, while the sweet breath of Heaven
      Was blowing on my body, felt within
      A corresponding mild creative breeze,
      A vital breeze which travell'd gently on
      O'er things which it had made, and is become
      A tempest, a redundant energy
      Vexing its own creation.
      The Prelude (1805), ed. Ernest de Selincourt and Helen Darbishire (London:
      Oxford, 1960), p. 2.
3.   *Walt Whitman's Leaves of Grass: The First (1855) Edition,* ed. and introd. Mal-
      colm Cowley (New York: Viking, 1959). All references appear in the text.

the much longer ones by Whitman, Emerson suggests some uniquely American matter:

> Our log-rolling, our stumps and their politics, our fisheries, our Negroes and Indians, our boasts and our repudiations, the wrath of rogues and the pusillanimity of honest men, the northern trade, the southern planting, the western clearing, Oregon and Texas, are yet unsung. Yet America is a poem in our eyes; its ample geography dizzies the imagination, and it will not wait long for metres. [37-8]

"The Poet" so obviously prescribes Whitman's later "metres" that the correspondences need not be belabored. What is important for the thesis of this book is Whitman's use of Transcendentalist ethics and metaphysics to establish his own sense of social value and personal identity — those qualities most strongly threatened by Negative Romanticism. Whitman is the most thoroughly egocentric of nineteenth-century writers. He is a man obsessed with establishing a sense of himself in relation to both the vastest kinds of cosmic order and the smallest forms of society, and Emersonian Transcendentalism provides him with the instrument for accomplishing his end.

In dealing with the 1855 *Leaves of Grass,* the first step is to come to terms with the self-portrait Whitman included as a frontispiece. An engraved daguerreotype, its pose sets the tone for both the book and Whitman's life work. The poet stands with his right hand on his hip and his left in his pocket, his head covered with a broad-brimmed hat slanted rakishly to one side. His eyes look with direct defiance at the reader, and his short beard is unkempt. Dressed in workman's clothes, he wears a shirt that is open at the throat, with his undershirt showing. The pose breaches good manners by the hand in the pocket, the hat on the head, and the open collar. The defiance in the poet's eyes, dress, and demeanor is Whitman's deliberate attempt to establish himself as something new in literature, as a poet of the American people, who never remove their hats, even for the president. His clothes are the uniform of a common man who is close to the life-giving earth, a man who says, "Don't tread on me." That Whitman took this kind of posing seriously is apparent from the fact that he continued to include pictures of himself in succeeding editions of *Leaves of Grass.* These portraits bear witness to his evolving sense of self — an evolution that culminated at last in the role of the ancient bard.[4]

4. See the portrait gallery in the Comprehensive Reader's Edition of Whitman's poetry, ed. Harold W. Blodgett and Sculley Bradley (New York: Norton, 1968).

It is clear from the Preface that follows his portrait that Whitman wished to be Emerson's poet, his American scholar, as a means of establishing his own identity. As a result, *Leaves of Grass,* even more than *Walden,* is a work in which the "I" is paramount. As in most Romantic works, the "I" is defined much more in opposition to, than in concert with society; even the supposedly conservative Emerson, for instance, had to renounce the conventional role of minister to become a virtuoso of the lecture platform.

I do not mean to suggest that Whitman merely played the sedulous ape. He goes much farther in many directions than Emerson would have dared, although this is a difference of temperament rather than of substance. The most obvious contrast between the two men can be seen in their definitions of the poet. For Emerson it is a role for *other* men to play, and the magisterial tone of "The Poet" shows a much more objective control than was apparent in *Nature.* Whitman, on the other hand, is not nearly so detached, for he always writes about himself. The poet described in the Preface is Walt Whitman all the way, a consciousness in search of an identity that can serve as a model for his readers. The self Whitman struggles to define goes beyond mere personality to seek roots in the hard surface of reality through which spirit manifests itself. And it is American facts that compose the central reality for Whitman's poet persona.

Whitman's America provides the finest poetic materials because it has turned the inheritance of the past into completely new forms. America is "essentially the greatest living poem." If Whitman's sense of the country differs from Emerson's, it is because their sensory orientations are dissimilar. Emerson's primary sense is visual, while Whitman's is tactile and kinetic. He is especially responsive to the "teeming" flux of America, and he wishes to redirect this inchoate energy. Whitman loves the unconventional "roughs and beards" on whom he models himself. He feels the overwhelming "space" of the American continent, loves its rugged lack of finish and its "nonchalance." The possibilities for "laziness" in America are crucial to him, because it is only with such "nonchalance" that one can "loaf and invite the soul."

Whitman finds "the genius of the United States . . . always most in the common people" (5-6) — a reminiscence of the frontispiece and a suggestion that the poetic role he is defining is really a self-portrait. Like most nineteenth-century men of letters, Whitman draws his democratic feeling from empathy. The American "bard is to be commensurate with a people" (6). He must know them intimately at all levels, most particularly that which is closest to the land. He must have an empathetic capacity that "responds to his country's spirit . . . he incarnates its geography and natural life and rivers and lakes" (7). The facts of his country, its people, its physical reality: a poet must absorb these in order to be commensurate with his people. And his "expression" must be "transcendent and new" (8).

But Whitman does not consider himself merely an *American* poet. For him the United States is a metaphor for the ideal situation in which a man can most adequately discover his transcendent self. Accordingly, America is not just *a* place, but *the* place, and the poet who will celebrate it is the quintessential poet.

Whitman understands, as does Emerson, the human need for a symbolic figure from whom the people can draw their identity and who can be, in Whitman's term, "the equable man." While Emerson's three representative figures are the Knower, the Doer, and the Sayer, Whitman now sees the Poet — Emerson's Sayer — as indisputably *the* representative man. The poet is at the center, and all forms emanate from his sensibility. He embodies the unrealized potentialities inherent in us all. With inflated, cosmic rhetoric Whitman describes his poet:

> The greatest poet hardly knows pettiness or triviality. If he breathes into any thing that was before thought small it dilates with the grandeur and life of the universe. He is a seer . . . he is individual . . . he is complete in himself . . . the others are as good as he, only he sees it and they do not. [9]

It is doubtful whether Whitman really believed that he himself fit such a picture — except, perhaps, at moments. Whitman has to be seen in the context of Transcendentalism, as trying to strike a balance between his self-knowledge and his poetic ideal. It was in those moments of transcendence, when duality disappeared and the universal breath flowed through his nostrils, that he undoubtedly felt himself an Emersonian "great man," breathing new life into forms and grandeur into simple facts.

Such an organic man must write organic verse. Emerson spoke in "The Poet" of "metre-making arguments," and Whitman echoes his

master in a passage worth quoting at length as the most succinct statement ever of the organic theory of poetry:

> The poetic quality is not marshalled in rhyme or uniformity or abstract
> addresses to things nor in melancholy complaints or good precepts, but is
> the life of these and much else and is in the soul. The profit of rhyme is
> that it drops seeds of a sweeter and more luxuriant rhyme, and of uni-
> formity that it conveys itself into its own roots in the ground out of sight.
> The rhyme and uniformity of perfect poems show the free growth of
> metrical laws and bud from them as unerringly and loosely as lilacs or
> roses on a bush, and take shapes as compact as the shapes of chestnuts
> and oranges and melons and pears, and shed the perfume impalpable to
> form. [10]

The artist must be free of any kind of institutionalized poetics or any
kind of diction that follows accepted "rules." Poetic decorum is an
institution imposed from without, and since the Transcendentalists
waged war on all institutions, it is no wonder that Whitman wanted
his poet to be disreputable, a "beard," one of the "roughs." By extension, only when a man can give up all the social amenities, ignore all
the precepts, conundrums, and shibboleths with which society makes
him so dangerously comfortable will he possibly be his own man. The
poet's task is to set all men free by setting himself free. That is why
his art must be personal in content, form, and tone. It must evoke a
deep response, for the artist is charged with changing the lives of his
readers. He must speak the language of the people, with no pretension
to artistic elegance. That this is more Whitman's ideal than his practice should be clear to any reader, for although the poetry often seems
just a series of direct statements, it contains so many prosodic conventions and uses of formal diction that they belie the theory Whitman
creates for his poet. This is not to denigrate his attempt, for much of
the diction and choice of subject matter is decidedly informal, and a
good case could be made that Whitman developed a new kind of
poetic line as well as a new use of spoken stress units as the rhythmic
pattern of his verse. Even Wordsworth, whose propaganda in behalf
of natural speech in poetry is more well known, was in actual practice
quite traditional in both form and diction, as Coleridge pointed out in
Biographia Literaria.[5]

---

5. See Sculley Bradley, "The Fundamental Metrical Principle in Whitman's Poetry,"
   American Literature X (January 1939), 437–59.

It is in choice of subject matter that Whitman is a great liberating force in Romantic poetry. Consistent with the Transcendentalist theory that meaning is universally immanent, everything in the world becomes grist for Whitman's poetic mill. Many early Romantic figures found science inimical to the imagination because of its penchant for analytically reducing phenomena. Wordsworth lamented in *Lyrical Ballads* that "We murder to dissect" ("The Tables Turned"). Poe's sonnet "To Science," in which science destroys myth, is yet another example of this attitude. But, by contrast, Whitman humorously shouts in *Song of Myself:* "Hurrah for positive science! Long live exact demonstration!" (47) And in the Preface he states:

> Exact science and its practical movements are no checks on the greatest poet but always his encouragement and support. . . . If there shall be love and content between the father and the son and if the greatness of the son is the exuding of the greatness of the father there shall be love between the poet and the man of demonstrable science. In the beauty of poems are the tuft and final applause of science. [14]

If, as Whitman notes, echoing Emerson, the poet is the one who can best describe reality and discern fact, then science, which is simply a more exact way of measuring the world, will never get in the way of the poet; it should, if anything, help him in comprehending reality and reaching beneath the merely measurable. The fact that both scientist and poet pursue reality leads Whitman to ascribe a love of precision as a poetic necessity. As much creative energy goes into a multiplication table or a steamboat as into any subject that poets normally celebrate. The most important task for any creative individual is to get down to first principles, to reach through the mass of irrelevant data to the noumenal reality that lies within.

Implicit in all of Whitman's ideas is the concept of political liberty, which becomes explicit more than halfway through the Preface. This concept follows logically from Transcendentalist assumptions. The thread of universal transcendence connects all men equally. And if all men are instructed to break away and set out together on the open road, then the systems under which their society operates must contain the democratic safeguards needed to protect their freedom.

> Liberty relies upon itself, invites no one, promises nothing, sits in calmness and light, is positive and composed, and knows no discouragement. [16]

Since the essence of liberty is spiritual, Whitman would undoubtedly call it a first principle because he defines the soul in much the same way a few pages later: "Only the soul is of itself . . . all else has reference to what ensues" (19). As a sine qua non of life, liberty is both self-contained and self-reliant, and yet the paradox is that all first principles exist in history. Both soul and liberty are definable, not just from their inherent qualities, but also by the history of their being, by the sum of events that have defined them in the past and will perpetuate them into the future.

It is ironic, although understandable, that the Transcendentalists are often accused of being ahistorical; to suggest that the world at any moment is the self-contained creation of a present moment of consciousness is to suggest that the past has little meaning. But among their many seeming contradictions, the Transcendentalists, including Whitman, have a strong regard for history, though they refuse to see it as a series of events with linear demarcations and readily ascribable causes and effects. They refuse also to venerate the past because such regard would turn it into another institution. The past matters in the ways it manifests itself in present consciousness, and the historic past is important largely because individuals always repeat the experience of some period of history; and so we have, as Emerson asserted in "History," our own Greek and Roman ages. Whitman explores the relationship of past and present in the following passage:

> these singly and wholly inured at their time and inure now and will inure always to the identities from which they sprung or shall spring. . . . Did you guess any of them lived only its moments? The world does not so exist . . . no parts palpable or impalpable so exist . . . no result exists now without being from its long antecedent result, and that from its antecedent, and so backward without the farthest mentionable spot coming a bit nearer the beginning than any other spot. [20-21]

Nothing is created in a moment *ex nihilo*. The only way to understand any entity is to understand its history. When Whitman states that "The direct trial of him who would be the greatest poet is today" (21), he is not dismissing the past. He only means that any poet who cannot deal with his own time cannot be a poet for any other. Nor can he know the past, for all time partakes equally of eternal truths.

The poet's task is to discover what is timeless and universal:

> A great poem is for ages and ages in common and for all degrees

and complexions and all departments and sects and for a woman as much as a man and a man as much as a woman. A great poem is no finish to a man or a woman but rather a beginning. [22]

A poem is for all men, and its timelessness opens the reader's perceptions into a new consciousness of life. When conceived in this way, poetry becomes a new religion, with the poet, the transcendent man, as the leader of the new faith. Whitman states his program directly:

> There will soon be no more priests. Their work is done. They may wait awhile . . . perhaps a generation or two . . . dropping off by degrees. A superior breed shall take their place . . . the gangs of kosmos and prophets en masse shall take their place. A new order shall arise and they shall be the priests of man, and every man shall be his own priest. [22]

The new religion of democracy will be led by the poets and universal men Whitman calls "kosmos." In this religion without a Church each person will discover his religious inspiration in the present time and in the "real objects" of the world, the "symptoms of the past and future." Without theogonic justification or rationalization, it will be a religion of total acceptance in the antinomian tradition of intuition and the inner light. Arising in the symbolic land of America, the new faith will "be responded to from the remainder of the earth."

The poet-priest of the new religion will lead all mankind to the open road, where he will preach his message in English because "The English language befriends the grand American expression" (22). That Whitman's own prose stretches the English language even in his Preface exemplifies his claims. He clearly saw himself as a poet-prophet who would lead nineteenth-century man out of the morass of despair into a new-found sense of personal and social identity.

> An individual is as superb as a nation when he has the qualities which make a superb nation. The soul of the largest and wealthiest and proudest nation may well go half-way to meet that of its poets. . . . The proof of a poet is that his country absorbs him as affectionately as he has absorbed it. [24]

For Whitman the Transcendentalist heroic redeemer is the visionary poet who expresses the national soul by embracing the nation. It is a role he prepared himself to play in the years before 1855, during his dandyish, bohemian days, when he frequented Pfaff's Beer Cellar, rode the streetcars and met thousands of people, edited liberal Democratic newspapers, and secretly prepared his poems and set them in type.

And it is a role he played with increasing relish throughout his life. The ancient bard positively breathes in the late Eakins portrait.

This self-conscious preparation was an important stage in the development of the Romantic ego in America, for Whitman was the only Transcendentalist to propose a truly innovative way for the self to reenter a violating society. Emerson simply did not go far enough and was always repressed by an innate conservatism. Thoreau, on the other hand, chose the role of outcast and antagonist, preferring to be a moral gadfly to his culture. Whitman alone found a positive way of playing a Transcendentalist role, by creating his own version of the "great man" without violating any of Emerson's basic principles. His buoyant optimism kept him from seeing that so total a reliance on intuition and universal good will has severe limitations, both practical and metaphysical. This insight was one that the "gloomy" Hawthorne and the "brooding" Melville shared.

4

THE ANTI-TRANSCENDENTALIST REACTION

Because Romanticism is in great part defined by its continually emerging historical process, one of the important threads any critic must follow is the dialectical pattern that characterizes the shifts between the various Romantic stages. The Hegelian movement from thesis to synthesis through antithesis is easily discernible by an examination of the intellectual movement from Analogism through Transcendentalism to the first stage of Realism. The problem of symmetry on which Analogism foundered was solved temporarily by the Transcendentalists' postulation of an all-encompassing sphere of spiritual value. But difficulties inherent in Emerson's vision were apparent to a number of mid-nineteenth-century writers who ultimately found that the values of Transcendentalism were illusory and that they contained no legitimate means by which the individual could make moral discriminations.

Both Hawthorne and Melville, in the two best-known American novels, almost parody Transcendentalism while seeking to set forth a new thesis that sees the world as existing primarily without intrinsic value and that finds the only possible source of human identity to lie in the unmediated confrontation between a metaphorically naked individual and a world seen without any illusions, a stripped-down universe without value. Both Hester Prynne and Captain Ahab are

Transcendentalists of sorts, portrayed seductively but ultimately the purveyors of illusion — for the Realists the primary sin. The self in the mid-nineteenth century is seen by the Realists as primarily a social construction, as a personality subject to consistent societal violation. The solutions of Thoreau and Whitman to the problems of self and role are wholly inadequate for both Melville and Hawthorne, who ultimately find all quests meaningless and survival the only adequate human goal.

This first stage of Realism I have called the Realist "impulse" to distinguish it from the later stage of realistic fiction that uses the philosophical insights of the Realist impulse and adds to it a corresponding style of direct presentation and ironic distance. Hawthorne and Melville are still, in the context of Realism, somewhat old-fashioned literary figures, who often write like the Transcendentalists their words damn. But their astringent critique is unmistakable.

Illusion and Role in *The Scarlet Letter*

As a novel of the emerging Realist orientation, *The Scarlet Letter* is concerned with two basic problems: the traditional Romantic dilemma of establishing a new relationship between the individual self and its social role; and the belief that men's illusions — their refusal or their inability to see the world as it really is — are the major impediments to their forging this relationship. Hawthorne could not accept the implicit assumption that there is a fixed connection between a society and its citizens, nor could he accept the Transcendentalists' assumption that the individual must break with society in order to establish his "freedom."

For Hawthorne, in *The Scarlet Letter* as in his early stories, man can achieve "salvation" only by realizing his inadequacy in either finding or creating meaning in the world. This realization, however, is only a beginning, for having recognized the impossibility of charging the world with meaning, the individual must come to terms with reality by looking at it without preconceptions, to see what it contains. He must, in addition, find a new way of participating in the social order and of redefining the premises that underlie his society's conception of human community. Society may be a mere convention of man, but it is necessary; and the moral foundation on which it must be rebuilt will be neither divine nor rational but will be based on an element all Romantic authors came to see as more important than either. Men band together for reasons of love as well as survival; therefore the "magnetic chain of humanity" must rely on the most important of all Romantic virtues: empathy, the deepest sympathy that can exist between individuals who have reached beyond role and personality to the self and to the selves of others. The Romantic community will rest on the foundation of such empathetic relationships. While in its abstract statement this belief may sound just like Whitman's statement, the differences between Hawthorne and the author of the 1855 Preface are quite marked. Their respective definitions of self differ radically, and Hawthorne feels quite differently about the individual's debt to his community.

In "The Custom-House," Hawthorne posits in some form or other all the views he will develop in the novel. With cautious irony he describes the role of the author:

> when he casts his leaves forth upon the wind, the author addresses, not the many who will fling aside his volume, or never take it up, but the few who will understand him, better than most of his schoolmates and life-mates. Some authors, indeed, do far more than this, and indulge themselves in such confidential depths of revelation as could fittingly be addressed, only and exclusively, to the heart and mind of perfect sympathy . . . we may prate of the circumstances that lie around us, and even of ourself, but still keep the inmost Me behind its veil. [3–4][1]

The author is an independent observer who must see the object as it is and present reality to his reader without benefit of a mediating vision that falsely places value within the world. He must, in fact, describe without fully revealing how he feels. This attitude runs solidly counter to the Transcendentalist assumption that the creative artist must bare his inmost self utterly in order to commune with the world-soul. Hawthorne dispenses with the "I" that Thoreau and Whitman celebrated.

It is no accident that Hawthorne discovers the papers of Surveyor Pue. A surveyor ordinarily measures, observes, and speculates, but he leaves the design and interpretation of materials and site to the architect. Hawthorne would like, at least so far as moral values are concerned, to be surveyor rather than architect of his materials and to

1. All quotations from *The Scarlet Letter* are taken from the Centenary Edition (Columbus: Ohio State University Press, 1962). All references appear in the text.

present his fictional reality in all its ambiguous complexity so that the
reader might draw his own conclusions. He knows the human desire
for certainty only too well, and only remittingly will he cater to it.
Every man must be architect of his own values, and no one can be the
final interpreter of any reality.

In this opening sketch Hawthorne wishes to show parallels between the Boston of two hundred years earlier and the Custom-House
of his own day. In each setting the individual must work out his destiny
in terms of a social role. By accepting a position as customs inspector,
Hawthorne acquiesced in playing a role that was defined by the state
and became ultimately a source of personal violation. To strengthen
the example of his own violation, Hawthorne conducts a census of the
empty characters who frequent the Custom-House.

These men have lost most of their interest in living; they awaken
long enough "to bore one another with the several thousandth repeti-
tion of old sea-stories, and mouldy jokes, that had grown to be pass-
words and countersigns among them" (14). General Miller is described as being "radically conservative," and the Inspector as a man
of "instinct" who seems to have "no soul, no heart, no mind." The
Collector, although he may have certain intellectual and spiritual
capacities, has nonetheless permitted himself to become an old fortress
covered with "grass and alien weeds." Only the "man of business"
strikes Hawthorne as "thoroughly adapted to the situation which he
held." Throughout his description Hawthorne does not condemn; the
irony of his slightly mocking tone carries the burden of judgment. He
too, after all, has allowed a social role to interfere with his life. While
working at the Custom-House he has been unable to write; and when
the administration by which he was appointed has been voted out of
office, he is happy to let a whim of fate secure his freedom, for the
fickleness of the spoils system sweeps him back to his real life's work,
that which is most closely connected with his "inmost me."

"The Custom-House" serves other functions for Hawthorne, not
the least of which is to allow him to develop a solid sense of historicity.
He tells of discovering the letter "A" among some old relics, an action
that establishes both the context of his tale and the reality of his chief
symbol. Like Melville, who took great pains to establish the reality of
the monstrous whale before presenting it to his readers, Hawthorne
recounts the discovery of the letter in order both to peg his tale in

history and to treat it as a legend which, although fictionalized, has at least an initial basis in fact.

Hawthorne then uses the essay to establish his split with Transcendentalism. After leaving his first tour of duty in the Custom-House, he had gone to live among the "dreamy brethren of Brook Farm." If he had had some doubts about the adequacy of Transcendentalism before going to Brook Farm (and "The Prophetic Pictures" and "The Minister's Black Veil" show that he had), he was confirmed in his belief by the time he left. The Transcendentalists were "dreamy" because they lived in the world of illusion rather than of fact. Connecting the dreamy Transcendentalists with the sleepy occupants of the Custom-House, Hawthorne avers in his essay that he could have reentered society on its own terms only by compromising his personal vision. Playing an unnatural role takes too much away from a man: "An entire class of susceptibilities, and a gift connected with them, — of no great richness or value, but the best I had, — was gone from me" (36). Ironically enough, both utopian social reform and official role-playing are self-isolating actions that fail to make him a part of "the united effort of mankind."

Rejecting not only Transcendentalism but all mediating visions, simple answers, and illusory hopes, the artist must look at the world directly in order to see human life for what it is. Even the simplest definitive assertion is a fiction he must discard and resist as much as the human drive for certitude will permit. Hawthorne begins by casting off the "figurative self." He decides to write as one beyond the grave, one who has accepted death — the ultimate, indeed the defining, reality of life. "Peace be with all the world! My blessing on my friends! My forgiveness to my enemies! For I am in the realm of quiet!" (44). With his recognition of human limitation, Hawthorne has gained a humility that enables him both to live and to create once again. Consonant with his discovery, he warns us in the first chapter that *The Scarlet Letter* will be "a tale of human frailty and sorrow" (48).

By setting his tale in Puritan New England, Hawthorne establishes himself as a Romantic historian. The search for ancient settings by nineteenth-century authors is more than a fashion whereby scholars today can recognize and pigeonhole a particular work as Romantic. Choice of setting is an essential part of Hawthorne's strategy because it permits him to control the environment in which he poses his thematic problem. Hawthorne's Boston is a fictional creation that depends on a myth of the quality of life when Massachusetts was a colony. Although his picture of New England is historically inaccurate in a number of details, Hawthorne assumes that the Puritan ethos contained a remarkably single-minded idea of the individual's obligation to his society. This unitive attitude toward the individual and society, even though it is based on the artist's assumption rather than on observed fact, allows Hawthorne to present a contemporary dilemma with much less confusion than would otherwise have been possible. The author's society is always too complex to be described with clarity, especially on an issue so emotional and varied. Hawthorne's purpose in creating a historical setting is much the same as was Melville's in creating an entire world on board a ship. Their shared purpose is not to retreat from current problems, but to present and confront them with greater precision.

Such precision is afforded by Hawthorne's narrator, who comments on historical Boston from the distance of two centuries. Taking advantage of this perspective, he begins at once to show the relativity of cultural values. When Hester stands the first time on the scaffold, Hawthorne makes clear how an observer ought to view the assumptions of her society: "a penalty which, in our days, would infer a degree of mocking infamy and ridicule, might then be invested with almost as stern a dignity as the punishment of death itself" (50). New Englanders are "a people amongst whom religion and law were almost identical," and their moral certainty makes them absolutely sure that all instances of adultery deserve severe punishment. But not only are social values conventional; the simplest appearances are deceiving in relation to which mediating vision an individual brings to his perceptions. Had "a Papist" been in the crowd, he might have seen Hester and her baby as "the image of Divine Maternity": one perceives reality according to his preconceptions.

One of Hawthorne's chief devices is his use of a fabular tone, which gives his story the moral authority of a legend. But the constant use of such circumlocutions as "it was said" or "it seemed" also puts perception on the level of a supposition. Critics have always had great difficulty in talking about Hawthorne's ambiguity because he avoids taking a stand on even the simplest kinds of perceptions. This annoying habit is nevertheless thematically central to his art.

Once it is understood that society's values are conventional, it becomes apparent that society's roles are equally limited. They are constitutive to neither a divine nor a rational order of things but are either imposed on the individual from without or accepted by him so that he may adapt. Society has forced the role of Adultress upon Hester. Granted, she has committed adultery; but it is one thing to commit an act that "had a consecration of its own" and another to accept a label. In order to remain within the community, Hester had no choice but to allow the town to establish her identity, but by the limited way she accepts the implications of her label, she ultimately points out the inadequacy of her punishment. Her scarlet emblem isolates her even as she stands on the scaffold: "It had the effect of a spell, taking her out of the ordinary relations with humanity, and inclosing her in a sphere by herself" (54). What could be a greater sin to the Puritan community than isolation?

Hester's stubborn individuality is made apparent in this scene as she stands on the scaffold and remembers her past life in England amid a family and society that seem in retrospect to have been happy and orderly. She recalls her marriage to Roger Chillingworth — a social union that is the highest institutionalized form of human relationship. At this moment of stress Hester might very well suppress a full realization of what is happening to her and retreat into a past that her memory endows with happiness and order. She might also accept the punishment offered by society and through a sincere repentance be led back to its bosom. Hester, however, neither lives in the past nor sincerely repents. Brought quickly back to full consciousness by the gaze of the crowd,

> She clutched the child so fiercely to her breast, that it sent forth a cry; she turned her eyes downward at the scarlet letter, and even touched it with her finger, to assure herself that the infant and the shame were real. Yes! — these were realities, — all else had vanished! [59]

The face of the community cannot be avoided. Hester accepts her punishment but rises above it, expressing an attitude of defiance by finally looking the people in the eye and not bowing her head to their stares. To face the world directly, neither imposing nor submitting to a mediating vision, is the philosophical ideal of the Realist vision and a precursor of the literary method later called Realism. It is Ishmael's ultimate conclusion in *Moby-Dick* that one should cease the folly of imposing a vision upon the world and should simply accept life as it is:

> I have perceived that in all cases man must eventually lower, or at least
> shift, his conceit of attainable felicity; not placing it anywhere in the in-
> tellect or the fancy; but in the wife, the heart, the bed, the table, the·
> saddle, the fire-side, the country.[2]

In May of 1861 Hawthorne wrote a letter to his friend and publisher,
Ticknor, in which he observed, "It is folly for mortal man to do anything more than pitch a tent" — a statement much in keeping with
Ishmael's and with the tone of Hawthorne's own novel of the previous
decade.[3]

Not only Hester, however, is affected by an arbitrary social role.
The effect is seen as well on Pearl, the result of the illicit union. Hawthorne never permits her an entry into "the magnetic chain of humanity" until her father acknowledges his paternity at the end of the novel
and admits her at last into the family, the simplest organic social unit.
Pearl remains an object even to those who love her because she is
forced into premature isolation. In spite of the reasons they give, the
Puritan leaders really want to take Pearl away from her mother because they are aware that a child must live in some positive relation to
his society in order to have a completed sense of identity.

Even further, Pearl, whose analogy to the scarlet letter is pointed
out more than once by Hawthorne, functions symbolically in the novel
as well as in Puritan society. She is the pure child, an unblemished
perceiver who is unburdened by adult illusions. Thus she can see the
world for what it is rather than for what it is supposed to be. She is, for
instance, unafraid of the witch-haunted woods. She sees through Dimmesdale and Hester when they refuse to acknowledge their union publicly. Nor will she permit Hester to discard the scarlet letter, into which
so much of Pearl's own identity is bound. It is not until Hester has
achieved *the right* to discard the letter that her child will permit her to
do so, and then only because Pearl's own right to be a human being
will have been acknowledged. Pearl is thus a victim of society's
assumption that it may impose roles on individuals and that its values
are divinely ordained; and she is a victim of her father's illusion that
he can use his role as a protection against facing reality.

2. Herman Melville, *Moby-Dick,* ed. Charles Feidelson (Indianapolis: Bobbs-Merrill,
   1964), p. 533.
3. Henry G. Fairbanks, *The Lasting Loneliness of Nathaniel Hawthorne* (Albany:
   Magi Books, 1965), p. 76.

Roger Chillingworth, Hawthorne's Gothic mad scientist, is yet another character implicated in the moral dilemma because he refuses to see the difference between self and role and because he asserts the kind of Transcendentalist individualism that Hawthorne found unwarranted. Chillingworth wishes initially to punish Hester because she has violated a social role he has imposed upon her. He cannot accept the fact that because he has been an unfit husband, Hester might wish to achieve with someone else an emotional union that goes beyond Puritan sanctions. He has actually forced her into sinning, but he hides behind the institution of marriage to avoid facing his own responsibility. Ironically, an institution designed to force moral restraint upon a man functions in this instance to shield him from a deeper kind of personal obligation. Chillingworth is thus no better than the society that condemns Hester. His appeal to "reason" and "truth" becomes a convenient escape from moral responsibility.

Chillingworth further "sins" by overusing his "mental" faculty. In asserting that neither the mind nor the will has limits, he is reminiscent of Melville's Ahab and, more important, of Emerson himself. During his prison interview with Hester, the physician's wife refuses to identify her lover. Chillingworth responds with overwhelming intellectual arrogance:

> "Never sayest thou?" rejoined he, with a smile of dark and *self-relying* intelligence. "Never know him! Believe me, Hester, there are few things, — whether in the outward world, or, to a certain depth, in the invisible sphere of thought, — few things hidden from the man, who devotes himself earnestly and unreservedly to the solution of a mystery." [75; italics added]

The attitude Chillingworth expresses here is strikingly similar in spirit to that of "The American Scholar" (1837):

> Help must come from the bosom alone. The scholar is that man who must take up into himself all the ability of the time, all the contributions of the past, all the hopes of the future. He must be an university of knowledges. If there be one lesson more than another which should pierce his ear, it is, The world is nothing, the man is all; in yourself is the law of all nature, and you know not yet how a globule of sap ascends; in yourself slumbers the whole of Reason; it is for you to know all; it is for you to dare all.[4]

4. *The Complete Works of Ralph Waldo Emerson,* ed. E. W. Emerson (Boston: Houghton Mifflin, 1904), I, 113–14.

Hester's reply to Chillingworth suggests the contradictions Hawthorne found lurking behind the seductive rhetoric of Emerson's Transcendentalism: " 'Thy acts are like mercy. . . . But thy words interpret thee as a terror!' " (76). Chillingworth overemphasizes the adequacy of reason and intuition; he is a man "accustomed to look inward, and to whom external matters are of little value and import, unless they bear relation to something within his mind" (61). But society, as blinded by its own illusions as Chillingworth is by his, cannot see beneath the surface that he presents. To them he is a doctor, a role they endow with social significance and moral value. Doctors, after all, are concerned solely with the welfare of their patients. How can they possibly be guilty of violating either the physical or the mental health of a patient? Since this judgment is implicit in the conventional category within which his society views Chillingworth, the citizens of the community cannot imagine for a moment what Chillingworth is in fact doing to Dimmesdale. Nor can Dimmesdale, blinded by the same conventions, see Chillingworth's true nature in time to protect himself.

Dimmesdale is both victim and manipulator of his social role. He uses his position to protect himself and to avoid facing publicly the real truth of his life. He is, after all, a minister of God and, by the social definition of his role, could not be guilty of an act such as adultery. Dimmesdale knows that the people will never see beneath his mask, and he uses his position shrewdly.

Not only does he protect himself by exploiting his role, he also violates at least two other people quite seriously by being unwilling to defy social convention and to face the world directly. By denying his personal responsibility, he forces Hester to bear the stigma of the scarlet letter, and by denying his paternity he prevents Pearl from becoming a fully realized human being. His symbiotic relationship with Chillingworth further saps the younger man. But the heaviest toll is the one the minister forces himself to pay. As he achieves steadily higher stature as a preacher, he withers emotionally as well as physically, much like Captain Ahab and that latter-day Ahab, Mr. Kurtz.

The most intense dramatization of Dimmesdale's continual dilemma occurs during the second of the three scaffold scenes, in Chapter 12. During the day the Reverend Dimmesdale can maintain himself through the built-in protections of the ministry, but at night, alone, he must go without its insulating armor; he even scourges his naked back.

In the second scaffold scene the isolated minister ascends the steps of the scaffold to acknowledge privately the guilt he must hide by day. The compulsion to confess, strikingly similar to Raskolnikov's in *Crime and Punishment,* is first manifested here.

This scene bothered Henry James in his study of Hawthorne because of its "want of reality and an abuse of the fanciful element." But James misses the author's intention, for Hawthorne's interest here is psychological; he is attempting to convey the state of mind of the shattered Romantic figure, totally alienated and unable to find value in either the world without or the self within. Trapped in his nightmare consciousness, Dimmesdale is the victim of his inner guilt and the attitudes bred into him by his society. He experiences a complete loss of identity. In no other scene in the novel does he feel a greater insecurity amid the shifting phenomena of the world. "To the untrue man, the whole universe is false, — it is impalpable, — it shrinks to nothing within his grasp. And he himself, in so far as he shows himself in a false light, becomes a shadow, or, indeed ceases to exist" (145-46). Existence means action; but Dimmesdale is paralyzed.[5]

Hawthorne divides the scene carefully into two parts. At first there are the appearances of Governor Bellingham, Mistress Hibbins, and the Reverend Mr. Wilson, each of whom represents one difficulty of Dimmesdale's situation — his inability to deal adequately with the state, with the threatening forces of darkness and moral chaos, or with the established Church. Wilson, for instance, passes by with his lantern "never once turning his head towards the guilty platform" (151), not even noticing Dimmesdale on the scaffold. Arthur Dimmesdale, the isolated individual, is intensely aware of the surrounding hostile world, but it recognizes him only in terms of his social role.

The second part of the scene foreshadows the remaining two stages of Dimmesdale's quest. He holds the hands of Hester and Pearl, and through this empathizing act he momentarily attains a sense of identity. He feels a "tumultuous rush of new life, other life than his own, pouring like a torrent into his heart, and hurrying through all his veins. . . . The three formed an electric chain" (153). This release of Transcendental forces from within the self is reenacted later in the brookside reunion with Hester. Yet Pearl's insistent demand for a public confession "tomorrow noon" points to the illusion of Transcenden-

5. Henry James, *Hawthorne* (London, 1879), p. 114.

talist adequacy that Dimmesdale must ultimately confront in the final
scaffold scene. As if to emphasize the need for a frank acceptance of
things as they are and the dangers of imposing false views upon life, the
"great vault brightened, like the dome of an immense lamp. It showed
the familiar scene of the street, with the distinctness of mid-day, but
also with the awfulness that is always imparted to familiar objects by an
unaccustomed light" (154). The light reveals the simple, implacable
objects of everyday experience, "but with a singularity of aspect that
seemed to give another moral interpretation to the things of this world
than they had ever borne before." From above, the three are seen on
the platform, metaphorically naked before the nighttime world, Hester
with her glimmering scarlet letter and Dimmesdale with his hand over
his heart. Pearl tries to make Dimmesdale look across the street, but
his face is turned upward to gaze, not upon a meteor, but upon the
letter "A." Dimmesdale still sees the world symbolically; for him the
sky is "no more than a fitting page for his soul's history and fate"
(155). His limited moment of true empathy and personal adequacy
has faded. It is impossible at night for Dimmesdale to deny his society's
values, but to accede in the light of day to Pearl's request for acknowl-
edgment is another matter, and one that Dimmesdale will avoid for
some time more. Chillingworth comes at last to take him home to be
the Reverend Arthur Dimmesdale. The man Arthur must once again
be suppressed.

It is not until he meets Hester by the forest brook that Dimmesdale can begin to break through to a new vision of possibilities and to
renew the sense of personal value and identity foreshadowed in the
earlier scaffold scene. The agent of this change is Hester, whose life
apart and solitary suffering have given her the time and stimulation to
think and to develop a self-reliant strength. In describing her state of
mind, Hawthorne suggests a kind of Transcendentalism:

> The world's law was no law for her mind. It was an age in which the
> human intellect, newly emancipated, had taken a more active and a wider
> range than for many centuries before . . . Hester Prynne imbibed this
> spirit. She assumed a freedom of speculation, then common enough on
> the other side of the Atlantic, but which our forefathers, had they known
> of it, would have held to be a deadlier crime than that stigmatized by the
> scarlet letter. In her lonesome cottage, by the sea-shore, thoughts visited
> her, such as dared to enter no other dwelling in New England; shadowy

guests, that would have been as perilous as demons to their entertainer, could they have been seen so much as knocking at her door. [164]

Hester has transcended her community by believing that her mind in its self-reliant individuality is free of the sanctions accepted by the majority of mankind. In so speculating, Hester comes dangerously near to the kind of specious freedom that Hawthorne was to condemn in such writers as Emerson and Alcott and in such characters as Chillingworth.

Hester's new vision, however, enables her to serve the town that had once dismissed and branded her as an Adultress. She becomes, as Richard Chase has noted, a kind of social worker. Moreover, she begins to realize that her silence has caused Dimmesdale immense suffering. In trying to protect him as a minister, she has helped to destroy him as a man. She realizes further that in protecting the identity of her legal husband, Roger Chillingworth, she has allowed the tacit obligations of that social role to stand between her and her love for Arthur. In their forest meeting Hester finally confesses this realization to Dimmesdale, and, after a momentary revulsion, he grants her his pardon.[6]

Hester's confession and Arthur's forgiveness are acts of empathy. They have stripped away the layers of role and personality to share a communion of selves, the highest Transcendentalist ideal. "Here, seen only by his eyes, the scarlet letter need not burn into the bosom of the fallen woman! Here, seen only by her eyes, Arthur Dimmesdale, false to God and man, might be, for one moment, true!" (195–96). Still, these realizations are possible only because Hester and Arthur are away from the sanctions of the community in the freedom of the forest — which is, ironically, condemned by the Puritans as a "moral wilderness." And indeed, they are correct in so calling it, because their social values cannot hold there.

Hester now calls on Dimmesdale to assume responsibility for their new insight; her appeal rests upon Transcendentalist illusions. " 'Leave this wreck and ruin here where it has happened! . . . There is good to be done! . . . Preach! Write! Act! Do anything, save to lie down and die!' " (198). Hester discards her scarlet letter, and the forest is bathed in sunshine. She undoes her cap and lets her hair flow

---

6. See Richard Chase, *The American Novel and Its Tradition* (New York: Anchor, 1957), p. 75. Chase talks of the " 'social-service' Hester."

freely for the first time in years. This reassertion of feminine sexuality is immediately reflected in her appearance. "A crimson flush was glowing on her cheek, that had been long so pale. Her sex, her youth, and the whole richness of her beauty, came back from what men call the irrevocable past, and clustered themselves, with her maiden hope, and a happiness before unknown, within the magic circle of this hour" (202). The forest itself seems suddenly transcendent, rising, as it were, in unconscious response to the joyful meeting of the souls of Hester and Arthur. Hawthorne comments: "Love, whether newly born, or aroused from a deathlike slumber, must always create a sunshine, filling the heart so full of radiance, that it overflows upon the outward world. Had the forest still kept its gloom, it would have been bright in Hester's eyes and bright in Arthur Dimmesdale's!" (203). The love that has pushed aside years of suppressed emotions seems to draw the two lovers from their social bondage. For the first time Arthur tries to reach out to Pearl as a father.

But Hawthorne permits both the reader and the lovers to maintain this illusion for only a little while. The discarded letter has landed by the far edge of the little forest brook, on the other side of which Pearl is playing. Water, in Romantic symbolism, frequently connotes time, change, and rebirth; and accordingly Hawthorne's description of the brook stresses these symbolic values. Now Pearl's image is reflected, dazzling and dancing, in the water as she points an accusing finger at her parents. Like the brook, Pearl is meant to remind the lovers of the past they would prefer to forget. In Pearl, Hawthorne unites the contradictions and complexities that the human orientative drive prefers to ignore: knowledge and ignorance, spirit and matter, beauty and deformity, the damned and the redeemed. Hawthorne emphasizes her symbolic role:

> In her was the visible tie that united them. She had been offered to the world, these seven years past, as the living hieroglyphic, in which was revealed the secret they so darkly sought to hide, — all written in this symbol, and all plainly manifest, — had there been a prophet or magician skilled to read the character of flame! [206–07]

This reference to flame, suggestive of the Biblical incident in which the twelve disciples receive the gift of speech, is an ambivalent allusion to Pearl's redemptive function. But Pearl offers neither a Christian nor any otherworldly redemption; she is reality, the truth about themselves that neither Hester nor Dimmesdale can hide. Only when they both acknowledge her and thus humanize her will they finally have accepted the basic facts of their lives and their destinies. All talk of escape and of self-consecrating love is illusion until reality is faced. This Transcendentalist illusion is no better than those they wish to leave behind.

Bowing to her daughter's accusing finger, Hester replaces the letter. The light that first bathed the scene now fades, and Pearl, alone as before, draws the light to herself. Hester's proposal is revealed as an escape from responsibility. The pact that she and Arthur Dimmesdale have made amounts to another act of self-deception, a judgment punctuated by Pearl's washing away the kiss that the false Dimmesdale has given her.

In this emotionally powerful scene, Hawthorne shows for the only time the passion that caused the adultery. He seduces the reader as well as the characters into believing in a solution to their dilemma. The seduction is deliberate, for Hawthorne has set up a situation in which there is no possibility of a happy outcome. He makes it obvious that his lovers have an obligation that prevents their escape. There is no avoiding responsibility to the community. The moment of illusion in the forest is the summit of Hester's role in the design of the novel. After this point she recedes steadily in importance.

To a point, Dimmesdale has shared Hester's vision along with her illusions. Because he feels his personal powers rising again, and because he has at least a rudimentary understanding of the split between his sense of self and his role as minister, he realizes the power that inheres in the conventional attributes of his social position. In the ecstasy of new insights and emotion, Dimmesdale is tempted to violate the trust of his parishioners. He wishes to denounce the validity of the communion supper to an old deacon. He almost denies the immortality of the soul to an old woman whose chief remaining comfort lies in religion. He is even tempted to soil the innocence of a young virgin who idolizes him. "The wretched minister! He had made a bargain very like [selling himself to the devil]! Tempted by a dream of happiness, he had yielded himself with deliberate choice, as he had never done before, to what he knew was deadly sin" (222). Entering his study, the minister puts aside the partly written election sermon and begins it once again. His new-found Transcendentalist vision has released a flood of creativity, although it has also made him at least partially aware of the dangerous and illusory authority it carries. He must play his final role supremely well before surrendering himself at last to public confession and death. Accordingly, his election sermon is a masterpiece.

Through this outcome Hawthorne introduces one of the book's most subversive ironies. He makes clear that it is possible to be a great public servant, a player of the most exalted and supposedly selfless role, with a flawed character, calculated deceit, and willful avoidance of self. Dimmesdale's value as a minister increases as the book continues, just as his body steadily wastes away. It is almost as though the consummate playing of a role can be nourished only by a corresponding destruction of self. At the end of the book, after the triumph of his election sermon, Dimmesdale seems to have reached the pinnacle of his calling. "Were there not the brilliant particles of a halo in the air about his head?" (250-51). If a redeemer ever had power to mold the thoughts and determine the actions of his people, it is Dimmesdale at this "proudest eminence of superiority" (249). "Each felt the impulse in himself, and, in the same breath, caught it from his neighbour. Within the church, it had hardly been kept down; beneath the sky, it pealed upward to the zenith" (250).

But the minister's Transcendental eminence is not enough. The hero of the Election Sermon must become the antihero of the final scaffold confession before he can achieve a true Romantic salvation. Ascending the steps with Pearl and Hester, he tears away the ministerial band and stands "with a flush of triumph in his face, as one who, in the crisis of acutest pain, had won a victory" (255), before he sinks to the floor, his life ebbing from him. His confession has made it possible at last for Pearl to "grow up amid human joy and sorrow, nor forever do battle with the world, but be a woman in it" (256).

The Scarlet Letter is ultimately Dimmesdale's book. He is the only character with the strength to face reality directly and still to accept his obligation to the community. It is not enough to admit failure privately; truth must be publicly acknowledged, made part of society's consciousness, so that the "electric chain" of humanity can be maintained. At the moment of her greatest self-awareness and compassion, Hester can suggest only escape. Chillingworth, who sees through society's pretensions, can use his insights only for the violation of others, much like the Duke and the King in *Huckleberry Finn;* his insights are therefore more than destructive; ultimately they turn back upon him with great irony. It is Chillingworth's constant working on Dimmesdale that reduces the minister to the state of anguish in which — and only in which — he can at last make his confession. When Dimmesdale does escape the power of the physician, the mad old scientist has no longer any inner resources on which to call and no further tasks to perform in the world. He soon dies.

Through Dimmesdale, Hawthorne rejects Negative Romantic isolation and alienation as well as Chillingworth's equally isolating rationalism. And through the minister, Hawthorne reveals the weaknesses of Hester's Transcendentalism, a position that Dimmesdale partially accepts but then builds on to go beyond any other character in establishing a new vision. Hawthorne further, through Dimmesdale, rejects the salvation seen in Transcendental love. For Hester, the recognition is painful. She cannot renounce the lovely Transcendentalist union in which she and Arthur might spend their " 'immortal life' " (256) together. But he has lost his illusions about love or death. Just as Tennyson had to escape from his dependence upon Hallam in *In Memoriam,* Dimmesdale must reject the reliance upon Hester he had felt in the forest when he said, "Think for me, Hester! Thou art strong. Resolve for me!' " (196). The genuine love that rises from empathy must not be submissive or dependent, exploiting or violating. In such an ideal relationship the lovers must retain reverence, says the dying minister, " 'each for the other's soul' " (256). Hawthorne comments in the "Conclusion" on the incredible ambiguities of strong emotion and on the difficulty of understanding the true face of the passions:

> It is a curious subject of observation and inquiry, whether hatred and love be not the same thing at bottom. Each, in its utmost development, supposes a high degree of intimacy and heart-knowledge; each renders an individual dependent for the food of his affections and spiritual life upon another; each leaves the passionate lover, or the no less passionate hater, forlorn and desolate by the withdrawal of his object. [260]

If distinctions between emotions so obvious and basic as love and hate can be no more than arbitrary, then how difficult must it be to see *anything* properly.

In the "Conclusion" Hawthorne returns finally to the themes he had first stressed in "The Custom-House": that the meaning of any experience can be known only to the individual and that, as an artist, the writer must simply tell what happened and what people thought it meant. Hawthorne uses the accounts of the final scaffold scene as his exemplum. Some witnesses thought that Dimmesdale punished himself for Hester's sin. Still others blamed the stigmata on Chillingworth's necromancy. Others saw the whole incident as a parable of the sinfulness of mankind. Hawthorne states that "the reader may choose among these theories" (259). He even claims that some of those present at Dimmesdale's death saw nothing at all on his breast. Hawthorne will not judge his characters so as to give his readers the false comfort of a "moral." To do so would be to impose value on reality, and there is never enough evidence about events to declare a conclusive verdict on anything. Conclusions are temporary and arbitrary, necessary only so that man may go on living. The author's advice is: "Be true! Be true! Be true! Show freely to the world, if not your worst, yet some trait whereby the worst may be inferred!" (260).

Both art and reality force us to choose, for the human orientative drive cannot remain forever suspended among alternatives. But art is a lie like everything else — with the difference, however, that it is the one "illusion" which, when used properly, can help man to look at the world with fewer illusions. Hawthorne knows that art will not reveal truth any more than does life. That is why he refuses to offer solutions. For the Realist, art is an instrument that warns against prating about the value of the world until we have experienced reality in all its horrifying and fascinating ambiguities. What Hawthorne finally thought about any of these matters is far from certain — as it should be, for while revealing so much and helping the reader even a little to face the certain uncertainties of his existence, he managed, as he promised in "The Custom-House," to keep his "inmost Me behind its veil."

The irony of Hawthorne's detached narrative tone is consistent with his refusal to commit himself for long to any normative position. Even though his diction often has an eighteenth-century formality and his nature description a strong hue of the sublime, his voice already looks forward to the ironic stance of one of his surprising disciples, Henry James, the chief theoretician of realistic fictional technique.

The Anti-Transcendentalism of *Moby-Dick*

The depth and scale of Melville's attack on Transcendentalism is almost hidden beneath *Moby-Dick*'s many-faceted surface. Great adventure story, symbolic allegory, the great epic romance of American industrialism, *Moby-Dick* fits all these labels and yet none of them. The most discussed of American books, it eludes all generic categories and defies conventional interpretation. Some of the immensity of Melville's novel becomes clear if it is examined against the background of Emersonian Transcendentalism.

I wish to suggest first that *Moby-Dick* is an almost ironic novel, perhaps even a parody. Although anti-Transcendental, it is, like *The Scarlet Letter*, written in the Transcendentalist style. A symbolic novel, its major "symbol" symbolizes absolutely nothing. Its heroic central figure is a character on the epic scale, whose strength totally overwhelms all the men who surround him; but he is blinded by his own vision, mouths the ideas of an author whom Melville thought "a humbug," and is ultimately a parody of the Transcendentalist "great man." The white whale whose image Captain Ahab pursues around the world is nothing but a whale—an occasion for the projection of symbolism but not a symbol. In any larger context the "Pequod's" quest means nothing and the fate of its crew signifies little. Whatever meaning the novel has lies in the paradigm presented by Ahab's quest and failure — all attempts to force meaning upon the world are futile; more than futile: they are destructive. The world exists. Physical reality is nothing more or less than what it is. Nature has no value; it wills nothing; its relation to man is one of coexistence.

By 1850, Transcendentalism was a long-established Romantic orientation, with Emerson its American spokesman. Melville, like Whitman, could absorb Transcendentalist ideas from the very air of his culture, but while he found the rhetoric often quite attractive, he strongly rejected the lessons Emerson was trying to teach. This is another case of an individual's discovering the contradictions inherent in an earlier orientation and proposing first a scathing critique and then a tentative new position. Melville quite clearly felt not only that Emerson had left many problems unsolved, but that he had failed even to take them into account. Melville's reaction to Emerson is instructive both in its insight and in its one-sidedness. The following summary of

Emerson's ideas as Melville might have understood them presents the side of Emerson most likely to have aroused the anti-Transcendentalist passion of Melville.

For Emerson the universe is a book that can be read by any individual: "Undoubtedly," he claims, "we have no questions to ask which are unanswerable" (I, 3). A spiritual reality underlies the world and unites both man and the vegetable in an occult relationship. "Nature always wears the colors of the spirit" (I, 11). Since the individual's origins are spiritual, he may feel free to extend his spirituality outward; this effort is limited for Emerson only by the size of the universe's spirituality. "Build therefore your own world," says Emerson. "As fast as you conform your life to the pure idea in your mind, that will unfold its great proportions" (I, 76). "The great man makes the great thing" (I, 105). He knows no master but his own will.[1]

If the "great man" has no ordinary limitations, then he must create for himself a new morality. Emerson states in "Self-Reliance" that "nothing is at last sacred but the integrity of your own mind." And further:

> No law can be sacred to me but that of my nature. Good and bad are but names very readily transferable to that or this; the only right is what is after my constitution; the only wrong what is against it. [II, 50]

It is just a short jump to "What I must do is all that concerns me, not what the people think" (II, 53); and to Ahab's shaking his fist at the sun, and asking, "Who's over me?"

For Melville the problems of freedom and of good and evil resolve themselves into one. Suppose, he seems to ask in *Moby-Dick*, the great man is not a good man? What then? Melville creates within his own context the greatest of all possible "great men," Captain Ahab. That such a magnificent figure — symbolic of a whole Romantic orientation — can indeed fail is Melville's judgment on the inadequacies of Transcendentalism.

Ironically, when he wrote *Moby-Dick*, Melville had not read Emerson. He had merely attended one of his lectures (5 February 1849), although he was by then familiar with his ideas, as were all innovative figures in American culture. That Melville was impressed by Emerson's presentation is clear from his correspondence with Evert

---

1. *The Complete Works of Ralph Waldo Emerson*, ed. E. W. Emerson (Boston: Houghton Mifflin, 1904). All references appear in the text.

Duyckinck. On 24 February he wrote, "I have heard Emerson since I have been here. Say what they will, he's a great man." A week later (3 March) he responded at more length:

> Nay, I do not oscillate in Emerson's rainbow, but prefer rather to hang myself in mine own halter than swing in any other man's swing. Yet I think Emerson is more than a brilliant fellow. Be his stuff begged, borrowed, or stolen, or of his own domestic manufacture he is an uncommon man. Swear he is a humbug—then is he no common humbug . . . I had only glanced at a book of his once in Putnam's store—that was all I knew of him, till I heard him lecture . . . Now, there is a something about every man elevated above mediocrity, which is, for the most part, instinctuly perceptible. This I see in Mr Emerson. And, frankly, for the sake of the argument, let us call him a fool;—then had I rather be a fool than a wise man.—I love all men who *dive*. Any fish can swim near the surface, but it takes a great whale to go down stairs five miles or more; & if he dont attain the bottom, why, all the lead in Galena can't fashion the plumet that will. I'm not talking of Mr Emerson now—but of the whole corps of thought-divers, that have been diving & coming up again with bloodshot eyes since the world began.
>
> I could readily see in Emerson, notwithstanding his merit, a gaping flaw. It was, the insinuation, that had he lived in those days when the world was made, he might have offered some valuable suggestions. These men are all cracked right across the brow. And never will the pullers-down be able to cope with the builders-up. [77-79][2]

In the opening sentence of the later letter Melville rejects the suggestion that he might be a follower of the Transcendentalist camp. And yet, although he does not approve of what Emerson has to say, he nonetheless find him "an uncommon man." Melville admires the figure Emerson cuts, not the words he utters. Emerson will take a chance; he is not just another pallid member of the intellectual elite. If there is something of the "fool" in Emerson, he is also "more than a brilliant fellow." Melville's feelings about the Concord lecturer are as ambivalent as those of Ishmael for his captain.

But it is Melville's imagery that is really striking. If Emerson is one of those men who dive, then he must be like "a great whale," for it takes an overwhelming creature to plumb the mysterious depths. Was he anticipating Moby Dick? But there is also "a gaping flaw" in Emerson that Melville will not allow his other qualities to obscure.

2. *The Letters of Herman Melville,* ed. M. R. Davis and W. H. Gilman (New Haven: Yale, 1960). All references appear in the text.

Emerson gave Melville an impression of high presumptuousness, a feeling that if he had been around when the world was created, he would have given God some good advice — perhaps even taken His place. Nothing in this impression is inconsistent with the ideas in Emerson, who always felt that each man contained divinity because all physical and animal reality emanated from divine spirit. Such men as Emerson "are cracked right across the brow." And who in *Moby-Dick* is cracked across the brow but Captain Ahab, with a jagged scar running from the side of his forehead down the side of his body? Once again, a prefiguring image. Obviously much of Melville's response to Emerson is in Ahab.

Melville identifies with the "pullers-down," for "builders-up" such as Emerson always try to project — with dangerous results — their own values onto the universe. The skeptical irony of the "pullers-down" is the only possible stance for Melville. The tension in *Moby-Dick* is between such a "puller-down," Ishmael, and Ahab, the "builder-up." Ishmael is a "puller-down" because he is a skeptic, because he attempts to see the universe as clearly as possible without projecting his own values upon it. Ahab is a "builder-up," like Emerson, in that he comes to his perception of the world with his mind already made up, and therefore he "builds up" the real world into something that reflects his own preconceived ideas as to what it means and contains. He is Emerson carried to the extreme — and the irony of his building-up is that it leads to another kind of pulling-down: the pulling-down of the "Pequod" to the bottom of the sea.

Before he saw *Moby-Dick* through its American publication, Melville wrote two famous letters to Hawthorne. Without mentioning Emerson by name, he discusses the problems of Transcendentalism at some length. In the first letter (April 16, 1851) he describes how, by turning words into symbols, men impose categories on the world.

> We incline to think that the Problem of the Universe is like the Freemason's mighty secret, so terrible to all children. It turns out, at last, to consist in a triangle, a mallet, and an apron. — nothing more! We incline to think that God cannot explain His own secrets, and that He would like a little information upon certain points Himself. We mortals astonish Him as much as He us. But it is this *Being* of the matter; there lies the knot with which we choke ourselves. As soon as you say *Me,* a *God,* a *Nature,* so soon you jump off from your stool and hang from the

beam. Yes, that word is the hangman. Take God out of the dictionary, and you would have Him in the street. [125]

Intellectuality, the imposition of mental constructs upon the universe, is a form of suicide. The "word is the hangman"; by categorizing any area of the world we limit our ability to see — and this is self-destruction. As Ishmael tells us of Queequeg's native island: "It is not down in any map; true places never are" (88). The only important measure of value is the accuracy with which the individual sees the world. Value lies in the confrontation, not in either the perceiver or the object, and the attempt to find value in the world or to see physical entities as symbols or retainers of meaning is a great mistake, a deadly mistake. When Melville tells Hawthorne that the Masonic mallet, triangle, and apron are nothing more than what they are, he is exhorting him not to be tempted into developing a new category of symbols. Avoid giving things names at all, if possible, and if not, then avoid letting names bestow finality or "significance" on the object. For names have nothing to do with "Being"; categories are antithetic to process, and the life process is ultimately the only reality.[3]

Moby-Dick is a paradigm of the above point of view. While it is certainly about the search for an albino whale, it is more certainly about the incredible dangers of myth-making. The whale symbolizes nothing. He is there, an occasion for others to create myths. Melville states as much in a chapter entitled "Moby Dick." Three generations of critics have busied themselves with worrying about what the whale symbolizes. They should have been concerned with the creator of meanings, Captain Ahab, for it is he, not Melville, who has created the "meaning" of the white whale. He fashions the myth of Moby Dick to give substance, form, and value to his own unhappy life, and he is aided in his efforts by other mariners who in turn project their own meanings onto the animal. His entire crew begins to share his vision, until the men are nothing more than instruments of their captain. When they agree to impose Ahab's arbitrary categories on the world, they give up their own free will — whatever that may be — and join him in a massive suicide. Narcissus sees his reflection in the pool and drowns trying to merge with it. In the first chapter Ishmael tells us that the meaning of Narcissus is "the key to it all"

3. *Moby Dick,* ed. and introd. Charles Feidelson, Junior (Indianapolis: Bobbs-Merrill, 1964). All references appear in the text.

(26). And he further admits that going out to sea and committing himself to the watery world is his "substitute for pistol and ball" (23).

In "Moby Dick" Melville warns us at length that the so-called symbolism of the white whale has been manufactured by ignorant sailors and a mad captain. The chapter begins shortly after Ahab, on the quarter deck, has enlisted the aid of the crew in his search. Ishmael admits that "a wild, mystical, sympathetical feeling was in me; Ahab's quenchless feud seemed mine" (239). He admits to sharing his captain's vision. The he begins to recount the growth of the Moby Dick legend.

Moby Dick has been widely known among whalers, although mainly through rumor; few sailors have actually seen him in the flesh. There have, however, been a number of recent incidents in the sperm-whale fishery "marked by various and not unfrequent instances of great ferocity, cunning, and malice in the monster attacked" (240). Ishmael emphasizes the superstitiousness of sailors and stresses that in their work whalemen come across "whatever is appallingly astonishing in the sea" (241).

> No wonder, then, that ever gathering volume from the mere transit over the widest watery spaces, the outblown rumors of the White Whale did in the end incorporate with themselves all manner of morbid hints, and half-formed foetal suggestions of supernatural agencies, which eventually invested Moby Dick with new terrors unborrowed from anything that visibly appears. [241-42]

Coupled with Moby Dick's "supernatural" aspect is the general range of myths surrounding sperm whales. Ishmael notes that even such great naturalists as Cuvier have believed these fantastic legends. Sailors who fish for right whales feel that "to chase and point lance at such an apparition as the Sperm Whale was not for mortal man" (243). When these myths are married to the prodigiousness of Moby Dick, the following is the result:

> One of the wild suggestions referred to, as at last coming to be linked with the White Whale in the minds of the superstitiously inclined, was the unearthly conceit that Moby Dick was ubiquitous; that he had actually been encountered in opposite latitudes at one and the same instant of time. [243]

If this sense of ubiquity is coupled with the seeming indestructibility that Moby Dick has displayed in his many encounters with whaling vessels, it cannot be much matter of surprise that some whalemen should go still further in their superstitions; declaring Moby Dick not only ubiquitous, but immortal (for immortality is but ubiquity in time). [244]

In the eyes of superstitious sailors Moby Dick has become a god, capable of ubiquity and immortality. Ishmael gives a lesson in how myths and gods are created; the other half of the lesson shows that an individual can respond to such a myth and use it as a projection of his disturbed mind.

On his previous voyage Captain Ahab had lost a limb to Moby Dick, who "reaped away Ahab's leg, as a mower a blade of grass in the field. No turbaned Turk, no hired Venetian or Malay, could have smote him with more *seeming* malice" (246; italics added). "Seeming" is the key word. To Ahab the whale "seems" malicious; but Moby Dick is no more malicious than he is godlike. His reaping of Ahab's leg is an animal's dumb, instinctive response to danger. In order to give himself significance, Ahab must imagine malice on the part of the whale. He feels chosen as the victim of fate, and his only response — given his nature — is to rebel outwardly and strike back at the universe, which he sees incarnate in Moby Dick.

> The White Whale swam before him as the monomanic incarnation of all those malicious agencies which some deep men feel eating in them, till they are left living on with half a heart and half a lung. [246]

> all evil, to crazy Ahab, were visibly personified, and made practically assailable in Moby Dick. [247]

Ahab's monomania demands that Moby Dick be more than a whale. He is "intent on an audacious, immitigable, and supernatural revenge" (251). For him the White Whale "might have seemed the gliding great demon of the seas of life." And the success with which Ahab is able to get the crew to share his projections of value onto a mute albino whale is stated by Ishmael in the last lines of the chapter:

> For one, I gave myself up to the abandonment of the time and the place; but while yet all a-rush to encounter the whale, could see naught in that brute but the deadliest ill. [252]

Ishmael, like the rest of the crew, comes to see the whale as Ahab wishes.

In the most famous lines of his April 16 letter to Hawthorne Melville writes:

> There is the grand truth about Nathaniel Hawthorne. He says NO! in
> thunder; but the Devil himself cannot make him say *yes.* For all men
> who say *yes,* lie; and all men who say *no,* — why they are in the happy
> condition of judicious, unincumbered travellers in Europe; they cross the
> frontiers into Eternity with nothing but a carpet-bag, — that is to say, the
> Ego. Whereas those *yes*-gentry, they travel with heaps of baggage, and,
> damn them! they will never get through the Custom House. What's the
> reason, Mr. Hawthorne, that in the last stages of metaphysics a fellow
> always falls to *swearing* so? I could rip an hour. [125]

Here he once again expresses his feelings about the "pullers-down"
and the "builders-up," calling them now the "*yes*-gentry" and those
"who say *no.*" Melville still stands, not on the side of those who would
project value onto the world or would tell how things are or should
be made, but with the skeptic who takes an ironic stance and carries
nothing with him but his ego, or sense of self. For he has now taken
an even stronger post-Transcendentalist position. The individual must
bring nothing to confront the world but his unfettered self. In order
to "get through" the Custom House, or the universe, it is necessary to
travel light, as Ishmael does. But if a man comes, as does Ahab, to
impose a vision, the customs inspector will never let him through.

Melville puts it more gently in the letter than in his novel. There
the yes-sayer or projector of value, Ahab, not only fails to make it past
the metaphorical customs house, he even leads an entire crew into
the doors of eternity. Ahab expresses figuratively the ideas stated in
Melville's letters, and it is through his example that Melville most
effectively discredits Transcendentalism and Emerson.

Emerson postulated a universe whose ultimate reality is a spirit
from which all of nature derives. All natural creations are therefore
equally endowed with divinity. If each person is potentially divine,
then the godlike in the individual man can be explored, exploited,
and developed, with no limitation other than the size of the universe,
which is infinite. There is no definable limitation or sanction on the
will of an individual who develops his potential divinity. The "great
man" has charisma. This quality was recognized and positively en-
couraged by Emerson and Whitman. Other men follow the "great
man" because he is the model for their own quest for greatness or,
at least, meaning. They are potentially he. This works well if he is
a good man as well as a great one. But with no sanctions, the man
of infinite will can do whatever he wants.

Ahab is the embodiment of Emerson's "great man," limited by nothing, privileged to do anything. His boundless hatred for the whale and sense of emancipation from conventional morality cause him to stand apart in the manner of the Transcendentalist hero.

> That inscrutable thing is chiefly what I hate; and be the white whale agent, or be the white whale principal, I will wreak that hate upon him. Talk not to me of blasphemy, man; I'd strike the sun if it insulted me . . . Who's over me? Truth hath no confines. [221]

Ahab's charisma is apparent in the very way the crew follows him many times in dangerous situations with a veneration bordering on worship and cosmic fear. A single word or gesture from their captain turns them from any thought of dissatisfaction or glimmer of mutiny.

But Ahab is not a "good" man. He has shut himself off from the most basic Romantic virtue — empathy. Even when his instincts lead him toward affection for and identification with another character — as in several confrontations with Starbuck and Pip near the end — he deliberately stiffens himself against his feelings. He tries to be all mind, all calculation. On June 1 Melville wrote to Hawthorne, "I stand for the heart. To the dogs with the head!" (129). Melville is on the side of heart and emotion; this statement to Hawthorne underlines the same attitude in the book. All of Ahab's *passion* is connected to his monomania; it is utterly one-directional and has nothing to do with *com*passion. He orders from the carpenter an ideal man with "no heart at all, brass forehead, and about a quarter of an acre of fine brains" (599).

Ahab is a figure of genuine magnificence, but in his delusions of a malign universe, embodied in Moby Dick, that has done him in, he uses his unchecked will to lead an entire crew to its death. In the nature of human relationships lesser men will follow a greater if he can supply their unconscious with the proper image. Emerson was right in this. But Melville contends that Emerson did not take sufficiently seriously the possibility that spirit could be anything other than "good." Although Emerson admitted the existence of evil, it was more than counterbalanced cosmically by a prevailing tendency to goodness in the collective actions of the world. He thus gave the impression to his contemporaries and to following generations that evil was of no great consequence in human events. By making Ahab the symbol of Transcendental magnificence, but by giving him the one flaw he felt that Emerson had not foreseen, Melville dramatizes this fallacy of the Transcendentalist position. Ironically, he accepts Emerson's prime image, while rejecting the value Emerson placed upon it.[4]

Melville's nay-sayer is Ishmael, who comes to the whaling ports in a state of deep depression and disorientation, lacking a sense of values to project upon the world. Indeed, his sense of identity is so stunted at this point that he must gain it from contacts with stronger men such as Queequeg and Ahab. Ishmael's stance is a peculiar blend of alienation and empathy. Because he lacks a strong sense of self (the primary sin for Emerson), Ishmael can understand the positions of all the characters in *Moby-Dick* but become permanently infected by none. To realize intuitively that man's greatest weakness is his need for illusion and to realize as well that any projection of meaning onto the world will result in illusion must finally mean a withdrawal from the traditional affairs of men to a kind of personal confrontation between the individual naked self and the world as naked object. Ishmael is the new post-Transcendentalist man, whose ultimate ironic detachment will become a commonplace pose for the new "hero" of the "realistic" novel.

Even the concepts of fate and free will that Ishmael proposes are consistent with Melville's total position. These ideas, stated in the chapter entitled "The Mat-Maker," are an attempt to avoid a fixed abstract stance. Neither fate nor free will as philosophical poles governs human events. Nor can one compromise a position by blending the two according to some formula and arriving at a set of regulations for running a life. The warp of necessity and the woof of free will still need "Queequeg's impulsive, indifferent sword" of chance to complete the pattern. Chance "has the last featuring blow at events." An unknown factor in the play of reality makes it impossible ever to describe or control it. Melville attempts to take a position that is in reality no position at all. No metaphysic is sufficient to account for the way things are; to this stage of Romanticism more than any other, all metaphysical systems are ultimately illusory. Ishmael therefore adds the final irony of chance, and Melville then exemplifies this position by having Ishmael's survival depend on an incredible series of coincidences.

4. See Emerson's essay "Compensation," from *Essays* (1841).

For instance: Queequeg decides he is going to die, and he requests that a coffin be built for him and it is; he then decides to live; a sailor falls from the mast and the original life buoy is thrown in after him and both sink to the bottom; Queequeg's coffin is then caulked and used as a replacement for the life buoy; on the second day of the chase Fedallah is dragged from Ahab's boat and killed; Ahab becomes harpooneer; the lead oarsman is put into Fedallah's place, and everyone moves up a notch; because Ishmael is in Starbuck's crew, he is on the "Pequod" rather than in another boat on the sea; on the final day of the chase he is picked to replace the oarsman on Ahab's boat; because he has the seat near the block, he is knocked overboard; since the chase goes away from him he can float free of the battle; when the "Pequod" sinks, he is just far enough away not to be sucked down in the whirlpool; and to help him float a day and night on the ocean is Queequeg's coffin, which, because it has been caulked to make a life buoy, has not sunk to the bottom along with everything else. None of these incidents is inevitable. They are all a matter of the most intricate and yet random kind of coincidence. Chance certainly "has the last featuring blow" at Ishmael. And that is the point. There is no figuring out why things happen — they just do.

But the most seductive danger of the Transcendentalist point of view is described best in Melville's June 1 letter to Hawthorne. It is the feeling that man is at one with the world:

> In reading some of Goethe's sayings, so worshipped by his votaries, I came across this, *"Live in the all."* That is to say, your separate identity is but a wretched one, — good; but get out of yourself, spread and expand yourself, and bring to yourself the tinglings of life that are felt in the flowers and the woods, that are felt in the planets Saturn and Venus, and the Fixed Stars. What nonsense! Here is a fellow with a raging toothache. "My dear boy," Goethe says to him, "you are sorely afflicted with that tooth; but you must *live in the all,* and then you will be happy!" As with all great genius, there is an immense deal of flummery in Goethe, and in proportion to my own contact with him, a monstrous deal of it in me. [130-31]

The "all" feeling corresponds to the Freudian "oceanic" feeling. The danger Melville felt in it, apart from its sentimentality, was that it deluded one into thinking life is comfortable and without danger. Throughout the book the readers are warned that to become unwary brings with it the danger of death. At the end of "The Mast-Head":

There is no life in thee, now, except that rocking life imparted by a gently rolling ship; by her, borrowed from the sea; by the sea, from the inscrutable tides of God. But while this sleep, this dream is on ye, move your foot or hand an inch; slip your hold at all; and your identity comes back in horror. Over Descartian vortices you hover. And perhaps, at midday, in the fairest weather, with one half-throttled shriek you drop through that transparent air into the summer sea, no more to rise for ever. Heed it well, ye Pantheists! [214-15]

It is possible without distortion to translate "pantheist" to mean Transcendentalist. Later on, in "The Try-Works," Ishmael is lulled into dropping his guard by the speeding motion of the ship and by the brightness of the fire that melts the blubber. He almost overturns the ship while he stands at the tiller immobilized. After finally recovering, he gives us this warning:

Look not too long in the face of the fire, O man! Never dream with thy hand on the helm! Turn not thy back to the compass; accept the first hint of the hitching tiller; believe not the artificial fire, when its redness makes all things look ghastly. [541-42]

Feelings of calm should alert men to the dangers of living that lie around the corner. But instead, for the early Romantic visionaries these "all" experiences were meaningful, "mystical" moments — meaningful in themselves and leading to no positive action other than sitting back and feeling "the tinglings of life that are felt in the flowers and the woods." Melville is quite aware of the attractiveness of the "all" feeling, for he writes in his second postscript of the June 1 letter:

N.B. This "all" feeling, though, there is some truth in. You must often have felt it, lying on the grass on a warm summer's day. Your legs seem to send out shoots into the earth. Your hair feels like leaves upon your head. This is the all feeling. But what plays the mischief with the truth is that men will insist upon the universal application of a temporary feeling or opinion. [131]

And yet, characteristically, Melville is quick to counter the attractiveness with a caution.

In Moby-Dick calm is always a mask for dark and mysterious terrors. Melville emphasizes the contrasts at the heart of existence, the calms at the heart of storms. On the day before Moby Dick's arrival, the sea and air seem quieter than ever. Melville does not claim that this is in the design of things, that there is a plan that makes these contrasts a part of the essential fabric of the world's structure. To the contrary, there is no design at all. The problem is that this mystical sense of oneness makes man relax just a bit too much. For Melville, man's prime virtue is his ability to perceive the world as object and to survive in it on the basis of his clear perceptions. If one feels so comfortable that he ignores the possibilities of danger inherent in just living in the world, he is in trouble.

After realizing that there is no profit in imposing value on a world without value, one must accept things as they are and retreat from the field of battle. In the ecstasy of sperm-squeezing Ishmael realizes the transience of his transcendent emotion:

> Would that I could keep squeezing that sperm for ever! For now, since by many prolonged, repeated experiences, I have perceived that in all cases man must eventually lower, or at least shift, his conceit of attainable felicity; not placing it anywhere in the intellect or the fancy; but in the wife, the heart, the bed, the table, the saddle, the fire-side, the country. [533]

This hope has at least some possibility of attainment, for it is tied to the physically tangible. The kind of quest undertaken by Ahab has none. Yet Ahab's quest is magnificent nonetheless.

Ahab creates Moby Dick, himself, and the fate of an entire crew. His grandeur derives from a supremely Wordsworthian and Emersonian imagination that unites itself in visionary union with the object:

> O Nature, and O soul of man! how far beyond all utterance are your linked analogies! not the smallest atom stirs or lives on matter, but has its cunning duplicate in mind. [406]

But Melville must reject this although, through Ishmael, he is ambivalent toward Ahab throughout the book.

Perhaps it is the imagination that must ultimately be condemned. Imagination must lead to illusion, as it does with Ahab. For that matter, so must art. And yet it is the use of imagination and will that led the earliest Romantics out of their sloughs of despond to seek value in the world. That has been the continuous paradox of all Romantic "solutions" until now. Imagination redeems, but it also destroys. For someone like Melville there is no choice left but lowering his gaze. That is why Ishmael concludes years after his experience in the book that retreat is the only possibility left for him; and that is why Melville retreated during the latter half of his own life. Retreat and acceptance, but no struggle. In Melville's final and most awful irony, Billy Budd goes to the yardarm blessing the name of his executioner.

For Melville the vast universe is indifferent. The universe he creates, whose king and whose inhabitants are taken so seriously for so many pages, is swallowed up quietly and quickly at the end, and nothing is left of the drama that has been enacted.

> Now small fowls flew screaming over the yet yawning gulf; a sullen white surf beat against its steep sides; then all collapsed, and the great shroud of the sea rolled on as it rolled five thousand years ago. [723]

To claim indifference for the universe is not to say that it is hostile. It is just to say that men should not conduct their battles against it. For these battles have no business being fought; they can never be won, since men are the only ones fighting. And yet, if pushed hard enough, the universe may, in recoil, destroy, or at least swallow. But if men wait long enough, it will swallow them anyway.

Moby-Dick is a book of almost total irony. For what it shows is that the most elaborate of "symbolic" tales has no real "meaning," except to demonstrate that things in general have no meaning; that the human quests have no function except as the most dangerous forms of diversion; that life is at its worst a struggle and at its best a surrender; and that the magnificence of great men and of works of art are only illusions that cannot capture reality because each creates a false one of its own.

In the vehemence with which it attacks all forms of illusion *Moby-Dick* is the great work of the first stage of Realism, and with its involuted irony and almost unresolvably contradictory tensions it looks ahead to such works as the later novels of Henry James and perhaps beyond them to Joyce and Faulkner. The philosophical stance it promulgates, along with that presented in *The Scarlet Letter,* serves as the foundation for almost all the later and more traditional works of literary realism.

5

REALISM AS VISION
AND STYLE

A number of interesting works have been written on the development of American Realism, notable among the more recent ones
books by Donald Pizer and Warner Berthoff, but the weakness of the
standard theories of American Realism derives from their tendency to
see the movement either too purely in a national or too much within
a literary context.[1]

Realism, as I see it, grows largely out of the continuing Romantic
dialectic. It is part of the Romantic movement and not distinct from
it. I have distinguished between the Realist "impulse" and the more
conventional concept of Realist style.

Realism as a philosophy derives heavily from the reaction against
Transcendentalism; it was proposed as a new synthesis prepared from
the contradictions in Emerson's vision. It suggests that the only value
possible in the world arises from the unmediated confrontation of
naked subject and naked object. Realist novelists finally see ironic
detachment as the only stance that can protect the "hero" or the
narrator of the novel. The development of Realism as an exact, almost
scientific, mode of describing the world goes hand in hand with the
need for writers to develop through both their narrative voices and
their characters sufficient protections against social and cosmic vio-

1. See Warner Berthoff, *The Ferment of Realism* (New York: Free Press, 1966);
and Donald Pizer, *Realism and Naturalism in Nineteenth-Century American Literature* (Carbondale and Edwardsville: Southern Illinois University Press, 1966).

lation. Irony is the new protective stance, a sort of mediating vision in its own right, that functions successfully until determinism becomes an overriding part of the equipment with which the later Realists see the world. At that point Naturalism takes over as the major vision in American letters, particularly in the works of Crane and Dreiser.

Huck's Ironic Circle

Twain's Huck Finn extends the implications of the Realist impulse into a unique mode of narrative presentation by employing a vernacular narrator of remarkable descriptive capabilities. Huck Finn sees, feels, smells, and hears everything, and although he often understands very little of what he perceives, he nonetheless speaks in a voice that is obviously "telling it like it is." Having dropped all the pretensions that informed much of Hawthorne and Melville's rhetoric, Twain, using Huck as his narrator, develops an almost perfect instrument for puncturing, through irony, many of his era's dominant illusions.

Huckleberry Finn has been badly misunderstood. It is not a novel about a boy's moral awakening, not a polemic against slavery, not a book about good instincts being stronger than an evil society. In those ways Huck Finn has been overestimated and his creator underestimated. It is now commonplace to lament that the book is best during the center section on the river and that Huck's stature diminishes in the passages dominated by Tom Sawyer. There is no question that Tom Sawyer overshadows Huck when they are together. The prose and the narrative structure are more controlled during the middle 200 pages. But neither Huck nor the moral dilemmas he has to face is understandable without the opening and closing episodes. For Twain has created an elaborate ironic structure that demands that the reader be taken in by his initial perceptions of Huckleberry Finn. The most important task of Realism was to destroy illusion. It is important that the reader be deceived, so that what happens to Huck later on will shock him into seeing that the problems posed in the book are unresolvable either in fiction or in life. He must not reject those parts of the novel that displease him or whitewash the ending into a demonstration of Huck's essential goodness, thus robbing Twain of his bite and his character of most of his fascinating complexity.

The dynamic theme throughout *Huckleberry Finn* is the unresolved dialectic between the moral responsibility of the individual and the morality of the society in which he moves and against which he must function. In *Huck Finn* a body of implied assumptions about property, human life, and human behavior is accepted without question by most of the "regular" people who live in the book's fictional country. To be "moral" in this environment is to act according to the community's legislated and unstated ethical codes, regardless of innate instincts or emotions. But underlying Twain's portrayal of Huck is the conviction that the morally responsible person acts according to his best instincts and to what *he* feels is right, regardless of what society thinks. Twain presents the first part of his dialectic directly through the inhabitants of his fictional South and the second by implication through a character who lacks the verbal tools needed for properly understanding the moral dilemmas to which he is subjected. The struggle can never be resolved because Huck does not know which side he is on. His upbringing has taken place far enough outside the society to maintain the sweetness of his natural instincts, but enough within it for him to have a "conscience." Huck *believes in* society and its repressive sanctions; at no point does he ever condemn the operations of the social order. Twain condemns them by implication, but Huck assumes that the shibboleths of property and propriety are self-justified. Ironically, Huck sees himself as a kind of outlaw next to Tom Sawyer, who was "brung up" right. Huck has never learned the good and proper ways of behavior, and he can therefore not expect any better behavior from himself. Whenever he breaks one of society's rules — such as setting Jim free — Huck knows he is wrong. The reader knows he is right, but Huck does not.

Since *Huck Finn* is a novel and not a tract, Twain introduces a brilliant literary device to complicate the moral issues and involve the reader in a constant dialectic with Twain the author and Huck Finn the narrator. This device is the deadpan storyteller, whom Henry Nash Smith has described as growing out of the frontier humorist who never cracks a smile at his own stories. Twain carries it a step farther, creating a character who not only does not smile at his own jokes, but does not even know they are funny.[2]

Because the stage comedian faces his audience directly, his listeners know his straight face to be a pose. But through the medium of the printed word and the conventions of written narrative, the writer is at a further remove from his reader and can thus play with the narrator and sit behind him pulling the strings. Huck Finn has no sense of humor. The fun in the book is all Twain's. All of Huck's remarks have a double edge: on one side Huck's seriousness, and on the other the underlying humor of implication that belongs to Twain. This ambiguity flatters the reader, too, because much as he may admire Huck, he knows that the reader is really a lot smarter than Huck. The reader is, indeed, as smart as the author.

To complicate matters further, Huck almost never makes a moral judgment. He is a magnificent observer, and it is a constant marvel how much he is able to notice and describe in his precise colloquial diction. But he never condemns any of the things the reader and Twain know to be morally reprehensible. In this sense Huck fulfills a Realist ideal by being the detached observer who sees everything and lets the facts speak their own message. The irony experienced here is that Twain judges by implication but never lets Huck make direct statements in support of what the author really feels.

By contrast, Tom Sawyer functions as the perfect representative of his society, made somewhat more palatable to the reader than are the adults because he is the conventional "bad boy." Although mischievous, he accepts without conflict the instinctive and intellectual values of his society. His boyish revolt takes the conventional forms of forming robber bands and running away, but they are only games to Tom, and it is understood that he will eventually become a pillar of the community who will remember with great nostalgia how he "cut up" when he was young. In the opening pages Tom forms his robber band. Huck Finn has finally sickened of the Widow Douglas's "sivilizing" ways and has left the respectable household in old rags to take up residence once again in his "sugar-hogshead." Huck says he "was free and satisfied. But Tom Sawyer, he hunted me up and said he was going to start a band of robbers, and *I might join if I would go*

---

2. See the Introduction to Henry Nash Smith's Riverside Edition of *Adventures of Huckleberry Finn,* which is even better than the chapter on *Huck* in Smith's celebrated book, *Mark Twain: The Development of a Writer* (Cambridge, Mass: Harvard, 1962).

back to the widow and be respectable. So I went back." [3; italics added][3]

Two items are of interest here. The first is the obvious contrast between a robber band and the requirement that its members be "respectable." Tom Sawyer could never contemplate being a robber if it meant living permanently outside the law, although Huck can empathize even with murderers. Playing robber is a sufficiently conventional boy's game. But, second, Huck immediately follows Tom's lead and returns to the life he dislikes. It must be remembered that even though he finds "sivilization" personally uncomfortable, he never condemns it. In Tom, Huck sees everything that is admirable in a boy who has the right upbringing and "a character." The passage quoted occurs at the very beginning, yet readers often display surprise when Huck assiduously follows Tom's lead at the end. Since Huck's self-esteem is so low, since he can say of himself, "I was so ignorant and so kind of low-down and ornery" (12), the reader should not be outraged when Huck does Tom's bidding. The irony is that the very elements Huck admires so strongly in Tom lead the reader through unmistakable implication to conclude that Tom is an unmitigated ass. But then, the reader is smarter than Huck.

All of Tom's behavior follows either a social or a literary model — which is exactly how society wants it. If all experience is controlled by codes and models, it is impossible for someone to step in with nothing but his instincts and intuition and act according to private morality. Spontaneity is unpredictable, and neither society nor its representative, Tom Sawyer, can tolerate the spontaneity of Huck. Tom's scheme for setting Jim free is the conventional literary medievalism of his time, and when Huck introduces his more efficient and simple ideas for getting Jim out, Tom accuses him of not wanting to do things "regular." Although Huck is occasionally out of patience with Tom, the worst he has to say is that Tom is "full of principle." He accepts the fact that his own ideas, although better, do not have the requisite style that only someone "brung up to it" can have.

For Twain and most of the Realists society is defined by precisely its emphasis on style and role-playing to the exclusion of the unpredictable. Social behavior is a vast complex of games and

3. *Adventures of Huckleberry Finn,* ed. and introd. Henry Nash Smith (Boston: Houghton Mifflin, 1958). All references appear in the text.

unexamined assumptions. In Twain's South property is an unquestioned imperative, and the designation of anything as property, be it
inanimate or black, grants an inviolable sanctity to the owner. Huck
has been trained enough to know this; he knows, for instance, that
when he is working to free Jim, he is doing wrong. His socially trained
conscience constantly overpowers his feelings, to the extent that twice
in the book Huck actually decides to turn Jim in. It is in the name of
property that he feels most guilt and waxes most moralistic. Jim confesses to Huck on the raft his aspiration to hire an "ab'litionist" to
steal his wife and children out of slavery. "It most froze me to hear
such talk," Huck says. "Here was this nigger which I had as good as
helped to run away, coming right out flat-footed and saying he would
steal his children — children that belonged to a man I didn't even
know; a man that hadn't ever done me no harm" (75). In Huck's
socially trained eyes the recipient of this injustice is the property
owner. What right has anyone to steal another man's property, even
if the "property" is his own wife and children?

All the institutions in a society cooperate to maintain its prevalent
standards. It is almost a commonplace since Marx (one of the most
important of all Romantic thinkers) to characterize the law as the
guardian of the status quo and to see it, not as the disinterested pro-
tector of all, but as the tool of those in power. Whether or not Twain
was so sophisticated in his thinking, Tom Sawyer, society's golden-
haired boy, gives the following rationalization for violating property
rights:

> It ain't no crime in a prisoner to steal the thing he needs to get away
> with, Tom said; it's his right; and so, as long as we was representing a
> prisoner, we had a perfect right to steal anything on this place we had
> the least use for, to get ourselves out of prison with. He said if we warn't
> prisoners it would be a very different thing, and nobody but a mean
> ornery person would steal when he warn't a prisoner. [203]

What marvelous legalism; how well Tom has learned his lessons.

As social institutions, both Sunday School and Church lend their
weight to protecting the divine right of property. Huck's skeptical
pragmatism constantly undercuts religion, but the finest use of this
kind of irony occurs the second time Huck contemplates turning in
Jim. The Duke and King have just sold Jim to the Phelpses, and Huck
is morally ambivalent about whether to write Miss Watson and turn

in Jim or whether to steal him from slavery. His head is filled with pulpit rhetoric before he makes his famous decision to go to hell, but the lines that follow show how strongly Twain indicts all of society's institutions for sanctioning slavery. A voice inside Huck keeps saying,

> "There was the Sunday School, you could a gone to it; and if you'd a done it they'd a learnt you, there, that people that acts as I'd been acting about that nigger goes to everlasting fire." [178]

Huck knows, without realizing the irony, that had he gone to Sunday School more often, he would have had the social code ingrained in him, with little possibility of his making a mistake or becoming involved in problems of conscience about which he would have to make an unaided moral decision. Religion, like all other social institutions (the nineteenth century realized increasingly that the Church was a social institution), protects property and the powers behind the status quo.

Aside from indicting social institutions for supporting a corrupt morality, Twain also demonstrates the power of a culture's overall assumptions to corrupt even the "good" members. Mr. Phelps is an obviously good and pious man, who seems to be totally without viciousness. A lay minister who has built his own chapel, he preaches (without pay) for the neighbors. He runs a house that the Lord has rewarded with prosperity, in which all blessings are shared generously. But he tries assiduously to return the slave Jim to his owner for a supposed $200 reward. Although he chains Jim to his bed in a dark shack, he feeds him well and even prays with him. When someone like Phelps, a truly good Christian in most of the best senses, places property values before humanity, it is clear how deeply the corruption is rooted.

The doctor who comes to treat Tom's bullet wound also shows a deep infection with the same diseases. Basically a good man, he is so concerned with protecting slave property that he will not leave Jim alone with the wounded Tom while he goes to fetch aid, for fear that Jim will run for his freedom — this is after Jim has remained selflessly by Tom's side for several days. The doctor's prejudice in behalf of property (he would surely never admit to being a racial bigot) prevents him from thinking logically, although he has enough fellow feeling to commend Jim to the townspeople as a "good nigger" — in return for which they promise to stop "cussing" him. Jim's selfless behavior in standing by Tom cannot be judged by the same standards applied to a white man's actions. Property and people are not the same.

Twain finds it just as insidious that society rewards style more than substance and that the typical mode of social behavior is the game — behavior acted out according to elaborate and unquestioned rules. For Tom Sawyer everything is a game. In human relations he reduces people to pawns on a chessboard. Even though he knows on arriving at the Phelpses' that Jim has been set free by Miss Watson's will, Tom is happy to keep him a slave for a while in order to play his elaborate masquerade of setting Jim free. For Tom style is more important than any other consideration, and he will violate other human beings continuously in order to follow the rules. Thus, with Huck's complicity, he puts Jim through a series of outrageous tortures. Huck's instincts tell him that Tom is wrong in doing so, and his pragmatic sense tells him that Tom's literary machinations are inefficient, but his "conscience" knows that Tom is right in his style although morally wrong in wanting to set free a slave. Huck does go along with Tom, willing to be an outlaw but unwilling to violate the proper sense of style and incur his friend's disapproval. On a seemingly harmless scale, this is a perfect imitation of adult behavior in that adults do almost nothing but play games.

Colonel Grangerford is the Southern aristocrat par excellence. He has the typical honorific title, dresses in white linen (prefiguring Twain's later uniform?), and maintains a household in which all the traditional amenities are observed, from gracious hosting to keeping a stable of slaves to religious piety and the ownership of traditional American bric-à-brac. He is an admirable figure in all respects, except for being head of a family that has for more than thirty years continued a feud with the Sheperdsons — another aristocratic Southern family — that is utterly bloody, inhumane, and mindless. It is an elaborate game with unquestioned rules. No one knows or cares how it began. When Huck asks Buck Grangerford about the meaning of the feud, he is answered with impatience. The feud is an established mode of behavior — indeed, a social institution — and it makes no difference how it began or what it means. Grangerfords kill Sheperdsons, and Sheperdsons kill Grangerfords. Each side has a real respect for the other; but the other side is distinctly the enemy. Like that of any other institution, the feud's main life force is self-perpetuation.

Twain has presented a model of wars as they are begun and sustained. He would no doubt have included the Civil War in this category; a. feud, like a war, is a game. But to call it a game is not to belittle its consequences, since in playing it, people are constantly killed. The only difference between adult games and those of children is that adults play for keeps; it is a matter of degree. Twain poses a problem that is central to the book and to the whole Romantic tradition. How can one, for long, live in and accept a society without playing its games? And having played them, how long can one remain in such a society without becoming permanently infected with its "morality"?

To add poignance and complexity to the question, Twain counterpoises against his society an individual who, for matters of personal survival, tries to escape it. Huck has to leave, not just because he hates "sivilization," but because Pap has locked him up and is beating him. Huck's feelings about "sivilization" are quite complex. Although society "cramps" him and he longs for his sugar-hogshead, he still has a great respect for the people who have "made it." He even adapts quite well, although slowly, to going to school and living with the widow.

> At first I hated the school, but by-and-by I got so I could stand it. . . . So the longer I went to school the easier it got to be. . . . The widow said I was coming along slow but sure, and doing very satisfactory. She said she warn't ashamed of me. [14-15]

Huck has a strong need to please others. Later, when he turns in the robbers on the reefed "Walter Scott" and thus saves the life of one of them, he also thinks of how it would please the widow:

> I wished the widow knowed about it. I judged she would be proud of me for helping these rapscallions, because rapscallions and dead beats is the kind the widow and good people takes the most interest in. [64]

The irony here is Twain's, not Huck's. Huck wants badly to please good people like the widow, although he wishes to have as little to do with them as he can. Even though Huck has at this point escaped successfully from society, he nevertheless cannot escape from the need to please the guardians of the order.

The truth is that Huck is not a genuine primitive; that role is reserved for his father. Toward the beginning, when Huck is with Pap, they catch part of a log raft that is adrift on the rising river — "nine logs fast together."

> Anybody but pap would a waited and seen the day through, so as to
> catch more stuff; but that warn't pap's style. Nine logs was enough for
> one time; he must shove right over to town and sell. [28]

The true primitive, like the aristocrat, does not postpone gratification.
Waiting is a middle-class characteristic. Immediate gratification, that
drink right away, is all that Pap worries about. It is Huck who understands postponement and who notices his father's primitiveness.

Huck shares the middle-class beliefs in the rights of property,
postponement of pleasure, and the necessity to please others. What he
has retained of his father's primitiveness is an impatience with clothes
and fancy housing, an intolerance of manners and uncomfortable customs (sitting still on Sundays, going to Church, and attending school),
a mistrust of cant (although a belief in it), and an intuitive sense of
social types (he sees through the undertaker at Peter Wilks's funeral)
and games — although he almost always sees the fault as being his
and not society's. It is this peculiar mixture that makes Huck's character so extraordinarily complex and Twain's overall point so difficult
to isolate.

On the raft Huck has the illusion that he has finally escaped from
the repressive sanctions of his society and can be "free and easy." Here
he and Jim can together shed their clothes and go naked. But their
action amounts to more than Leslie Fiedler's implications of homo-
sexual miscegenation, even at its most latent. The later nineteenth-
century impulse toward Realism was more than a literary method. It
was an effort to shed the overriding mediating visions that had grown
up since the Renaissance to replace the dying Christian ideology. From
the Enlightenment through the Transcendentalist movement there had
been a number of attempts to locate a source of meaning and identity
either in the empirical world or in an almost neo-Platonic spiritual
realm. *Moby-Dick* can be read as a brutal rejection of Transcendental
pantheism, although in it Melville still retained the Transcendentalist
style. As a later product of the same impulse, *Huckleberry Finn* is
written in the spare prose that has come to be associated with "realism." The new ethic is based on the direct confrontation by the individual with the world of fact, image, immediacy. Meaning is to be
discovered neither in the perceiving consciousness nor in the world,
but in the meeting of the two — both stripped naked. Contrasting the
views of nature in Twain and Whitman, it is clear that nowhere does

Twain attach the "mystical" significance to the external world that Whitman in his Transcendentalist overview must do. Huck often finds the world marvelous, but *for itself,* and the rest of the time the reality outside himself is simply an arena in which Huck must constantly attempt to solve the problem of being his own man.[4]

What better way of dramatizing the world and the self in naked confrontation than by stripping Huck and Jim of their clothes? Both Carlyle and Thoreau claimed that clothes were the emblems of social roles. The roles endemic to both Huck and Jim are those of free man and black man, master and slave. But stripped of their clothing on the river, floating free of landed social sanctions, the only relationship possible between them is that of two men in mutual confrontation, without the mediating vision of society to dictate their behavior. Their nakedness makes possible the constant empathy, highest of all Romantic ethical virtues, that flows between Huck and Jim. Indeed, it shows how, in special circumstances, the hard fact, the specific image, will triumph over the mediating vision of the social code. When Huck decides to do the "right thing" and turn Jim in to Miss Watson after Jim has been sold by the Duke and King, his thinking, as Henry Nash Smith has shown, takes on a kind of pulpit diction. The voice of religion tells him that "the plain hand of Providence" is "slapping me in the face" and "there's One that's always on the lookout." Thereupon he thinks about the Sunday School and then kneels down to pray — a conventional way of dealing with problems of morality. But his socially trained conscience is not clean, and he realizes he "can't pray a lie." He does the "right" thing and composes the note to Miss Watson; before he goes to post it, however, he thinks awhile and prepares himself to pray again, this time with a clear conscience. But his memory plays a trick on him. He recalls his trip down the river with Jim, the black *man.* He recalls the moonlight and the storms and their "floating along, talking, and singing and laughing." He remembers how Jim "would always call me honey, and pet me, and do everything he could think of for me"; and after that he can neither pray nor turn Jim in, but must now "decide, forever, betwixt two things." He decides, of course, to go to hell, to opt for the life of the "criminal,"

4. See Leslie Fiedler, *Love and Death in the American Novel,* rev. ed. (New York: Stein and Day, 1966), which covers primarily the same ground originally adumbrated in his essay, "Come Back to the Raft Ag'in, Huck Honey!" in *An End to Innocence* (Boston: Beacon, 1955), pp. 142-51.

at least in the eyes of his society — whose values *he does not reject*.

What has made possible the decision that Huck knows is immoral and that the reader knows to be highly moral is that the hard fact, the unmediated world Huck has discovered with Jim on the raft, has overcome the mediating vision, the ideology of society. Here is Twain's major moral point: The only way to overcome the manifestly evil customs of organized society is to strip down the self to face the world and other human beings directly. One must look clearly beyond the self and confront whatever is out there.

Twain has complicated this seemingly standard nineteenth-century literary morality with an irony that has been constantly misunderstood. The rest of the book shows that, although the highly moral state Huck achieves in his decision to go to hell is an ideal for the individual, it is also, like most ideals, impossible to maintain. Huck's falling off from this step of almost Transcendentalist goodness is not Twain's failure of vision, but his further feeling that the forces of society are stronger than the individual's will or his ability to maintain a constant naked confrontation with the world.

The highest moments of Huck's friendship with Jim occur on the raft away from the landed community; here they have no responsibilities to anything but themselves and their own survival. This state, however, cannot last. No one can live outside the social order indefinitely. The first prefiguring of this implication comes with the invasion of the raft by the Duke and King. As con men, they bring on board enough of the grasping venality of the land to show that they are really a part of landed values carried to an extreme. Society has followed Huck and Jim even out on the river, giving a first instance of the true inevitability of the social system.

The King and Duke operate by turning stock responses against the sheep of society. At the revival meeting the King uses conventional religious emotions to fleece the congregation. At Pokeville they both exploit the townspeople's thirst for the salacious in order to take them over. In Peter Wilks's town they manipulate the standard attitudes toward death and mourning to con the dead man's family out of his fortune. Through these role-players par excellence the book conducts its most savage indictment of the social order, although Huck never really condemns them and Twain does so only by implication. And yet, even though the two outrageous but lovable rascals finally get their comeuppance, Huck's sympathies go out to them as he sees them tarred and feathered and ridden out of town on a rail. His instinctive empathy is much stronger than any sense of righteous indignation — a social luxury and an emotion about which Huck knows little. The townspeople's brutality reflects the corruption of society as much as does the behavior of the King and the Duke.

The absolute surprise, however — even though the Duke and King are something of a preparation — is Huck's complicity in Tom Sawyer's outlandish scheme to free Jim. How could Huck, whose morality has been so patently demonstrated, engage in such an action? The truth is that he could have acted in this way all along had the circumstances been right. He has never condemned society or condemned slavery, he has always admired Tom Sawyer disproportionately and patronized blacks (even Jim on the raft), and he has not really been changed by his experiences on the river. This is not a *Bildungsroman,* and Huck Finn has not undergone a moral transformation. It is wrong to insist that he has.

Huck *does* love Jim. But it is only possible for him to feel the emotions for a "nigger" that he might feel for anyone else because he and Jim have left the scene where their interaction was controlled by the socially imposed roles of master and slave. Nonetheless they both carry with them their inbred attitudes. Jim never forgets that he is a "nigger" and that Huck is white. Huck constantly patronizes Jim in his thoughts, saying that you can't teach a "nigger" anything or that Jim is pretty smart "for a nigger." He does not understand that a black man can feel about his family the same way white people do. When Jim mourns the loss of his wife and children, Huck comments, "I do believe he cared just as much for his people as white folks does for their'n. It don't seem natural, but I reckon it's so" (131). Twain is, of course, implying that black people have feelings, but Huck cannot really believe it, much as he likes Jim.

At the end Jim is reduced almost to a parody of the ever-faithful, long-suffering, mindless, and stupid darky. This reversal has disturbed many readers, who insist that Jim is more noble than Twain finally permits him to be. But once again, it is a matter of circumstances. Jim can show great nobility when he does not have to play the slave. Once, however, he is returned to an environment in which the role is forced on him again, he reverts to his lifelong training. Even on the trip down the river Jim has not lost his slave traits. His well-developed sense of inferiority is demonstrated by his stated willingness to accept more abuse from white men than from black and by the pleased surprise in his voice when he states that Jack, Huck's slave at the Grangerford's, is "a good nigger and pooty smart."

It is with the friendship of Huck and Tom, however, that Twain makes his major ironic point about how little, if at all, Huck changes. What Huck admires most about Tom is his sense of style, for it is style that shows the degree of a person's adaptation to his role. Because Huck is so lacking in social self-esteem, he can admire someone like Tom, who is so comfortable and self-assured. Throughout the book Huck invokes Tom Sawyer at key moments, claiming either that Tom would really have done something up with style or that he would have been proud of the style Huck manages to work into a particular action. Huck is never completely his own man, and he never shakes the behavioral model of Tom Sawyer. The only difference on the raft is Tom's absence. It is therefore not surprising that on Tom's return Huck reverts to a kind of discipleship; he has been a disciple all along.

The first shock occurs when Huck tells Tom he is going to try to steal Jim. Tom says enthusiastically, "I'll *help* you steal him!" Huck responds with consternation:

> Well, I let go all holts then, like I was shot. It was the most astonishing speech I ever heard — and I'm bound to say Tom Sawyer fell, considerable, in my estimation. Only I couldn't believe it. Tom Sawyer *a nigger stealer!* [189]

It doesn't matter that he, Huck Finn, is setting free a slave. *He* was brung up wrong; because he knows no better, he has opted for the outcast life; he has chosen to go to hell. But Tom Sawyer is another matter.

> Here was a boy that was respectable, and well brung up; and had a character to lose; and folks at home that had characters; and he was bright and not leather-headed; and knowing and not ignorant; and not mean, but kind; and yet here he was, without any more pride, or rightness, or feeling, than to stoop to this business, and make himself a shame, and his family a shame, before everybody. I *couldn't* understand it, no way at all. It was outrageous. [196]

Tom is everything Huck thinks he himself is not. Therefore Huck is annoyed with Tom for doing something as lowdown and ornery as

Huck might do. It is Huck's reaction to Tom's willingness to free .Jim that, more than anything else, shows his attitude toward property and slavery to be unchanged.

Being a pragmatist, however, Huck is willing to accept the help and leadership of someone who has know-how and style. He welcomes the help of the young man with the proper literary models. Even when Twain is most ironic toward Tom, Huck never sees through the ridiculousness of his schemes except to say that he is a little "full of principle." Further, Huck can accept Tom's help because he is back on the stable land and is no longer troubled by the immediate problems of survival. He can become a little boy again and imitate adult games because with the Phelpses he is safe. This so-called "regression" is troubling; but Huck has always reacted in this way around Tom, with whom his adventures can be make-believe and never have to be "real." Tom sits on Huck's native instincts, and the latter's ironic veneration for society's ways forces him to obey its rules when he is safely within its bosom. Tom's rules are society's rules, his games a model of society's fantasies, his hypocrisies an image of the only ways society thinks it can be truthful to itself.

Throughout all the incredible machinations of setting Jim free, Huck is never easy about why Tom is helping him. Indeed, his very security in knowing that society is right is shaken. Huck is finally set at ease when he discovers that Tom knew all along Jim was a freed man and that Tom is therefore not guilty of violating the sanctity of property. That Tom is guilty of hypocrisy and willfully violating another human being is not apparent to Huck; these are accepted ways to act in the society in which he was raised. Notes Huck:

> and so, sure enough, Tom Sawyer had gone and took all that trouble and bother to set a free nigger free! and I couldn't ever understand, before, until. that minute and that talk, how he *could* help a body set a nigger free, with his bringing-up. [242-43]

There should no longer be any doubt as to Huck's feelings about slavery and the will of society. Nor do these events violate what has gone before, because Huck's attitude is both prefigured and continuously exposed.

At the end Tom suggests that the two of them "get an outfit, and go for howling adventures amongst the Injuns, over in the Territory, *for a couple of weeks or two*" (244; italics added). Like all good citi-

zens, Tom Sawyer contemplates antisocial activities only when they
are strictly limited in time. In other words, for Tom, to escape from
civilization is only another conventional game — he does not really
mean it. However, in the last lines of the book, Huck's famous words
are:

> But I reckon I got to light out for the Territory ahead of the rest, be-
> cause Aunt Sally she's going to adopt me and sivilize me and I can't
> stand it. I been there before. [245]

For Huck the escape is real because civilization cramps him; he does
not play games with his freedom. The irony of the book has now come
full circle, in that Huck has not rejected society's standards at all. He
simply feels personally inconvenienced by such aspects as school, Sunday School, and clothes. But Huck still believes just as strongly that society is right, and he shows that the only way to maintain even the
limited freedom that he really wants is to run away. On the last
two pages, then, Tom invites Huck to a good middle-class boy's game
while Huck desires strongly to escape the constricting amenities of the
community.

And the same relationship obtained on the first page of the book.
It is part of a pattern established right from the start. Neither character has changed. This irony has proved almost impossible for readers
to accept. And yet Twain's point would be so much weaker without it.

Twain has shown that society will almost always bend the individual to its ends and turn him into a cog in the wheel, a role in its
collective make-believe. For him the only way to avoid being destroyed
by civilization is to maintain a kind of radical innocence and to be, like
Huck, an ironic outcast. But Huck does not realize that there is irony
in his actions. He does not consciously perceive anything wrong with
society. Otherwise he might have turned out like the Duke or the King.
Because Huck's instincts are so often at variance with what he knows
to be right (and the reader knows to be wrong), he is really two people.
But more completely, Huck acts according to the situation, one way
within the social order and another outside it. It is therefore important
that Twain both begins the novel within society and ends by returning
to it. The middle section is the most attractive because, at least in part,
it is the most seductive. In it Twain can, in a series of episodes, point
out all the ills of a society and can show how attractive life is when
lived outside it. And yet he knows that escape is only temporary, that

sooner or later one must return and make his peace with the established order. Can one, however, return without being destroyed or turned into just another social cretin?

Twain never answers the question. The novel as the greatest realistic and ironic art form has never found it its task to answer questions; it has always satisfied itself with raising them. Twain poses a problem, posits a possible solution, gives it partial success, and then shows the failure of even a distinct possibility. There are no facile solutions to complex problems. To believe anything else is to believe an illusion.

Huckleberry Finn experiences direct confrontation, but he cannot shake the mediating vision that sees society and its values as instrinsic to the very nature of the universe. The innocent individual can function quite well with a minimum of social stress, but something more is needed for him to combat the day-to-day trials of living in a community. Huck's failure shows that man must learn how to reenter society even though he has found it necessary to leave for a time: if he does not learn, the social order has its own ways of retrieving him. But Twain does not tell how to make this reentry and retain wholeness as individuals. To give such an answer would be to promulgate an illusion, and that would be to abandon the Realist's basic responsibility.

Daisy Miller and the Social Octopus

Daisy Miller, although its scope is so much smaller, is basically concerned with the same problem as *Huckleberry Finn* — that of an "innocent" individual who is trying in some way to protect his individuality against a repressive society that thinks its behavioral rules absolute. In *Huck Finn* the innocent character survives by unwittingly adopting an ironic stance that allows him to remain in the community and yet not be violated by it. Daisy Miller, however, lacks both Huck's irony and his flexibility, and she is destroyed by her attempts at independence.

The narrative devices used in the two books are quite distinct. Twain lets the central character tell his own story, endowing him with a highly active consciousness and imagination, allowing the reader to see through his ostensibly naive eyes the shams and pretensions Huck perceives without understanding them. Further, since *Huck Finn* is often broadly comic, Twain uses his narrator to make the reader laugh at whatever he wishes to criticize. But *Daisy Miller,* while still comic both in the Balzacian sense and in its ironic tone, is more restrained and finally somber. Daisy does not tell her own story. James uses a limited third-person narrator who presents the tale through the consciousness of Frederick Winterbourne, a member of the society that Daisy allows to destroy her. But he assigns to Winterbourne a strong dose of ambivalence, so that throughout the story he wavers between an outright condemnation of Daisy's behavior and a freely emotional response to her charm and beauty. This ambivalence is crucial because it allows Winterbourne to dramatize the tension that James wishes to portray most strongly: between the individual who tries to stretch out freely and spontaneously and the repressive society that has evolved a stringent, unwritten code of behavior to ameliorate the nothingness of human life. Because Winterbourne's perceptions are central, and because he struggles so consciously with his ambivalence, it is he who emerges as the book's central character, rather than Daisy Miller. But like Huck Finn, he ends up exactly where he began. James's story describes another ironic circle.

The narrative consciousness that tells the story is best defined by its tone, which is ironic, urbane, and sophisticated. With detachment the narrator thrusts a pointed wit at his characters to show his moral superiority to them. When he describes Mrs. Costello's son, after the horrible mother and her sick headaches have already been introduced, he makes it clear that the son shares the narrator's opinion of the lady:

> This young man was amusing himself at Hombourg, and, though he was on his travels, was rarely perceived to visit any particular city at the moment selected by his mother for her own appearance there. [IV, 155][5]

This kind of calm, wordy cleverness conveys a sense of moral and sociological authority. The narrator establishes this on the first page, when he details the habits of Americans at European watering places,

5. *The Complete Tales of Henry James,* ed. Leon Edel (Philadelphia: Lippincott, 1962); this reproduces the first English edition of 1879. All references appear in the text. I have intentionally avoided using the New York Edition, since the revisions James made in 1908 reflect the sensibility of the later Stylist rather than that of the Realist of the 1870's. The original subtitle of *Daisy Miller* was "A Study"— possibly an indication of James's intention to be a student of society in this story.

and particularly of young American girls in their "muslin flounces." The reader is treated as an intelligent creature who is quite capable of understanding the narrator's wit but who is in some need of instruction as to social distinctions.

James chooses to begin with a description of the social setting because it is only within this environment that the particular problems of Daisy and Winterbourne could arise. The parts of Vevey and, later, of Rome that are introduced are peopled by wealthy Americans trying to establish a cosmopolitan society in which they can think of themselves as basically European but to which they nonetheless bring a rigidly Puritan moral sense. For them, social behavior has developed into an ossified pattern of moral absolutes; what one does in any situation is known beforehand and not to be questioned. Life becomes a ritual of acting out what everyone already knows to be good and proper, and middle-aged women sit like self-elected Furies waiting for someone to slip. In one exchange at Vevey, Winterbourne attempts to make a case for the Millers, but he meets stiff resistance from his aunt:

> He immediately perceived, from her tone, that Miss Daisy Miller's place in the social scale was low. "I am afraid you don't approve of them," he said.
> "They are very common," Mrs. Costello declared. "They are the sort of Americans that one does one's duty by not — not accepting." [155]

The rules of such a society are so closed that one does "one's duty" by refusing even to *meet* people like the Millers. Mrs. Costello is not conflicted; she *knows* what to do in all cases. Even Mrs. Walker, who is somewhat more patient, makes it finally explicit to Daisy that she must not walk the streets of Rome with Giovanelli, and when Winterbourne wavers, Mrs. Walker gives him no choice but to leave Daisy and join her in the carriage. Later, at her party, Mrs. Walker turns her back on the incorrigible girl and leaves her speechless.

The brash and uncultivated Millers are not sufficiently "civilized" to feel awe in the face of European "culture." They have little patience with ruined castles or with involved manners. Nor do they realize that behavior must be varied in a new environment. The little boy is obnoxiously jingoistic, the mother is unconscious in almost every way imaginable, and the father is an unseen presence — like Mrs. Newsome in *The Ambassadors* — back home in Schenectady making his money. Daisy is the only visible Miller who shows any complexity. This complexity is a combination of naive innocence, a refusal to let a morally constricted world of values that is foreign to her sensibility violate her in any way, and a streak of rebelliousness that denies her Huck Finn's flexibility and makes her fight each battle against the social order as though it were complete capitulation to give in to it in any way. Daisy is pretty, but her sensibility is somewhat common and her manner of social intercourse, because it does not conform to the manners of the society she is visiting, strikes both the people she meets and struck the readers of James's day as that of a contemptible flirt. But these opinions, like most moralistic judgments, are too easy, and they deny Daisy's complex humanity and her emotions.

Winterbourne quite definitely belongs to the society of Mrs. Costello and Mrs. Walker. His manners are at home in that ethos, but his sympathies are torn because he still retains the capacity to respond with an openness of feeling that leads him occasionally to flout the code of behavior to which he is morally beholden. The social order must control all aspects of the individual's behavior if it is to make him function successfully within it. It must teach him to categorize all people and all activities so well that no spontaneous feeling can lead him to act unpredictably. During each encounter with Daisy, Winterbourne's preceptions lead him to two insights: a consciousness of the charm of Daisy's naivete; and a consciousness of how she should be judged by a member of his social class. He spends a great deal of fruitless energy trying to reconcile these elements held in tension.

The story begins with Winterbourne visiting Vevey from Geneva, where he has been "studying" and is rumored to be spending time with a mysterious lady. He meets Daisy Miller quite by accident, after bumping into her little brother Randolph. When Daisy comes, Winterbourne is aware that he needs an introduction before he can speak to her, and yet he feels at the same time a freedom to dispense with that formality:

> In Geneva, as he had been perfectly aware, a young man was not at liberty to speak to a young unmarried lady except under certain rarely-occurring conditions; but here at Vevey, what conditions could be better than these? [145]

Daisy's manner leaves him quite nonplussed because it exhibits none of the coyness and distance a lady of her "station" ought to affect. Instead, her glance is "perfectly direct and unshrinking" (147), and she shows a thorough lack of ability to understand any customs other than those by which she was brought up. This is a condition curiously similar, at least in its ignorance, to that of her detractors in Vevey and Rome. She says, " 'The only thing I don't like . . . is the society. There isn't any society; or, if there is, I don't know where it keeps itself' " (150). Daisy does come from "society," but from a small-town society in upstate New York — a society in which the sexes mingle more freely and where flirtation is an accepted mode of behavior. But because these behavioral patterns do not obtain among the Americans in Europe, Daisy cannot recognize that these expatriates constitute a "society." Mrs. Costello, on the other hand, cannot believe that anyone who behaves as Daisy does can possibly come from "society." It would be a standoff, if Mrs. Costello did not represent all of the moral power in her own environment. They are, after all, not in Schenectady.

As for Winterbourne, he simply does not know how to react:

> Poor Winterbourne was amused, perplexed, and decidedly charmed. He had never yet heard a young girl express herself in just this fashion; never, at least, save in cases where to say such things seemed a kind of demonstrative evidence of a certain laxity of deportment. And yet was he to accuse Miss Daisy Miller of actual or potential *inconduite,* as they said at Geneva? He felt that he had lived at Geneva so long that he had lost a good deal; he had become dishabituated to the American tone. [150-51]

But he is aware of a certain cultural relativism, of the fact that there is an "American tone" as well as a European one, and that one ought to be cautious about too stringently applying the canons of a limited taste. In this consciousness he shows himself more complex morally than either of the two judging ladies. Nevertheless, Winterbourne does hunger for more certainty in categorizing this pretty girl. Is she a serious coquette or merely an American flirt? But he decides that coquettes are both sophisticated and predatory, and surely Daisy Miller is

> very unsophisticated; she was only a pretty American flirt. Winterbourne was almost grateful for having found the formula that applied to Miss Daisy Miller. [151]

Winterbourne feels secure with Daisy only after he has found the formula for reducing her to a category to which he will know how to respond. Seeing her as only a harmless flirt allows Winterbourne to continue the relationship, and although he cannot fathom her sudden changes in mood and demeanor, he can now feel safe in talking to her.

But Mrs. Costello is not so troubled. She makes moral decisions with all the indecision of a meat cleaver. She informs her nephew that it is their duty *not* to accept the Millers, that Daisy has an "intimacy" with her courier, that she is indeed nothing but a "dreadful girl!" Winterbourne, still a young man without a fully formed social consciousness, "listened with interest to these disclosures; they helped him to make up his mind about Miss Daisy. Evidently she was rather wild" (156). In the absence of his mother, Mrs. Costello gives her nephew an education in tribal morality. She warns him: "You have lived too long out of the country. You will be sure to make some great mistake. You are too innocent" (157). With this remark James plants one of the seeds of his broad dramatic irony.

Although Winterbourne takes his aunt's warnings to heart, he is strangely smitten by this girl whose whole mode of behavior he is obliged to reject. And yet, the preconceptions he realizes he must accept about Daisy allow him to respond to her as a curiosity rather than as a human being, and he can enjoy her without any reciprocal responsibility. The conflict between Winterbourne's instinctive response and his preconceptions can be pointed out by the following judgment:

> "Common," she was, as Mrs. Costello had pronounced her; yet it was a wonder to Winterbourne that, with her commonness, she had a singularly delicate grace. [161]

That someone of the category "common" can also be part of the category "graceful" is difficult for Winterbourne to fathom, so strongly does he accept Mrs. Costello's preconceptions. The reader must realize that Winterbourne has received his biases from his culture and not from his experience in the world apart from it; and like most people, he accepts these "formulas" as a way of avoiding moral judgments. The conflict between morality and moral responsibility is similar to that in *Huck Finn*.

When Winterbourne arrives in Rome the following winter, he is intrigued by the idea of seeing Daisy again, and he raises the subject with his aunt. Mrs. Costello informs her nephew that the vulgar Americans are carrying on quite badly there, just as they had in Vevey, only now " 'The girl goes about alone with her foreigners' " (172). Mrs. Costello once again concludes that "They are very dreadful people."

> Winterbourne meditated a moment. "They are very ignorant — very innocent only. Depend upon it they are not bad."
> "They are hopelessly vulgar," said Mrs. Costello. "Whether or no being hopelessly vulgar is being 'bad' is a question for the methaphysicians. They are bad enough to dislike, at any rate; for this short life that is quite enough." [172]

In this society, vulgarity is equivalent to evil. While this view may seem somewhat extreme, one of the major insights of Realism holds that all societies reify their codes of permissible behavior into moral absolutes, all the more strongly in the absence of belief in external sanctions for these values. Societies are man-made constructs, instruments originally of self-protection but turned very quickly into institutions of self-perpetuation, as Thoreau had long since pointed out, and like all institutions they are interested primarily in controlling human behavior.

Both Winterbourne and Mrs. Costello are right. The Millers are ignorant because of their innocence. They are not really aware that the suave Giovanelli is a gigolo ready to marry an American bank account. But it is also true that they are vulgar because they are so unconscious of the social discriminations that govern the milieu in which they have chosen to move. Were they to cease caring about the approval of those in the American colonies in Europe, they would be in better faith with their actions. It is not possible to be a rebel on the inside of a situation and then complain when others object to the behavior. The only way to bring off genuine social independence is to cease caring about approval and to act without concern for those who judge. But this level of detachment is beyond the Millers' capacity.

Winterbourne's problem is that he is too committed to his society to be able to make independent judgments. At best he can have more patience with Daisy's "bad behavior" and hope to bring her around; but he can never really believe that there is lasting value in her naivete and spontaneity. These are simply traits she must be trained away from. That is why, when Mrs. Walker tries to stop Daisy from walking with Giovanelli on the Pincio, Winterbourne takes Mrs. Walker's part, and when Mrs. Walker gives him her ultimatum, Winterbourne leaves

Daisy and gets into the carriage. Having reestablished her control (in the name of society) over Winterbourne, Mrs. Walker can then let him go back to Daisy, secure in the knowledge that he will not do anything foolish. Winterbourne suggests, "I suspect, Mrs. Walker, that you and I have lived too long at Geneva!" (186), but there is little danger that he will act on his insight. He knows who is boss.

Winterbourne is so sober, so stiff, that it does not occur to him at any time that Daisy might be hiding her true feelings, that her strange behavior is something he must simply accept, and that she might in some way be attracted to him more than to Giovanelli. Winterbourne tries to explain matters to her at Mrs. Walker's party:

> "Well," said Winterbourne, "when you deal with natives you must go by the custom of the place. Flirting is a purely American custom; it doesn't exist here." [191]

But Daisy rejects his advice, saying that at any rate Giovanelli is not preaching to her. For spending the evening with Giovanelli she is rewarded by Mrs. Walker's turning her back on her at the door. Daisy is for the first time perceptibly hurt by the insult, and Winterbourne reproaches Mrs. Walker mildly. When he later hears malicious gossip about Daisy,

> He felt very sorry for her — not exactly that he believed that she had completely lost her head, but because it was painful to hear so much that was pretty and undefended and natural assigned to a vulgar place among the categories of disorder. [196]

But Winterbourne does not question the verdict leveled at Daisy. Rather, it is his sensibility that is offended, because he cannot reconcile the contrast between the "vulgarity" of the judgment and the beauty of its object. Once again he tries to reason with Daisy when he finds her walking with her Italian companion. She, in turn, shows that she does care what people think about her:

> "Of course I care to know!" Daisy exclaimed seriously. "But I don't believe it. They are only pretending to be shocked. They don't really care a straw what I do. Besides, I don't go round so much." [199]

Daisy shows both her need to be taken seriously and her inability to accept the fact that the judgments society levels against her are really meant as seriously as Winterbourne suggests. She then accuses him of not protecting her more, and he responds by claiming that he does defend her. Mrs. Miller has told him that she believes Daisy to be engaged to Giovanelli. She then teases him once more:

> "Since you have mentioned it," she said, "I *am* engaged." . . . Winterbourne looked at her; he had stopped laughing. "You don't believe it!" she added.
> He was silent a moment; and then, "Yes, I believe it!" he said.
> "Oh, no, you don't," she answered. "Well, then — I am not!" [200]

When Winterbourne leaves her he is still thoroughly confused and unable to believe that Daisy might be doing more than simply teasing him. Because he has categorized her as an "American flirt," he cannot think that there is anything more to their relationship than the few characteristics permitted by that category.

Winterbourne's ambivalence achieves a temporary resolution, however, a week later, when he walks to the Coliseum late one night after a dinner party, to discover Daisy sitting there with Giovanelli. He is at last able to fit her totally into a category:

> Winterbourne stopped, with a sort of horror; and, it must be added, with a sort of relief. It was as if a sudden illumination had been flashed upon the ambiguity of Daisy's behaviour and the riddle had become easy to read. She was a young lady whom a gentleman need no longer be at pains to respect. [202]

His horror is really relief because at last the "ambiguity" is solved; Mrs. Costello and Mrs. Walker have been right all along. No "innocent" girl would be out at this time of night, unchaperoned, with a man, and at the Coliseum, the source of "Roman fever." It is always a relief not to have to make moral decisions. For the first time Winterbourne is strongly assertive, telling Daisy in no uncertain terms that she must go home, and reproaching Giovanelli severely for exposing his *innamorata* to serious illness. As they are leaving, Daisy asks Winterbourne. " 'Did you believe I was engaged the other day?' "

> "It doesn't matter what I believed the other day," said Winterbourne, still laughing.
> "Well, what do you believe now?"
> "I believe that it makes very little difference whether you are engaged or not!" [203]

This is the strongest reproof that Winterbourne has dealt her; he makes it clear that she has been relegated to the category of indifference. She is now simply a young girl he knows and does not respect, even though he might like to protect her from malaria. Daisy expresses her shock and even despair at this realization when she and Giovanelli leave in their carriage: " 'I don't care,' said Daisy, in a little strange tone, 'whether I have Roman fever or not!' " (204). If Winterbourne rejects her, then she no longer cares to live. She is silly and overly dramatic, but she is also desperate.

This interpretation of Daisy's despair is emphasized when she becomes mortally ill with malaria. On her deathbed, as she goes in and out of delirium, she gives her mother a message for Mr. Winterbourne:

". . . she told me to tell you. She told me to tell you that she never was engaged to that handsome Italian. . . . Any way, she says she's not engaged. I don't know why she wanted you to know; but she said to me three times — 'Mind you tell Mr. Winterbourne.' And then she told me to ask if you remembered the time you went to that castle, in Switzerland." [205]

Mrs. Miller does not know why Daisy was so insistent about the message; nor does Winterbourne. But by this time the reader knows. He understands now that Daisy has, in her unique way, been in love with Winterbourne, or has at the very least been totally dependent on his approval. But Winterbourne has been so trapped by his formulaic judgments that he can no longer respond to Daisy outside his categories.

At Daisy's funeral Winterbourne meets Giovanelli, whom no one has seen since Daisy fell ill. Giovanelli tells Winterbourne that Daisy " 'was the most beautiful young lady I ever saw, and the most amiable' "; and then he adds, " 'and she was the most innocent.' " This statement comes as a shock to Winterbourne, who asks, " 'And the most innocent?' " But Giovanelli confirms this: " 'The most innocent!' "

After Winterbourne reproaches him for taking Daisy to the Coliseum, Giovanelli says:

"If she had lived, I should have got nothing. She would never have married me, I am sure."

"She would never have married you?"

"For a moment I hoped so. But no. I am sure." [206]

Even then Winterbourne shows no immediate realization, but the following summer he meets his aunt at Vevey and tells her that he had done Daisy an "injustice." He now shows that he understood Daisy's feelings about him when he adds,

> "She would have appreciated one's esteem."
> "Is that a modest way," asked Mrs. Costello, "of saying that she would have reciprocated one's affection?" [206]

What a tortured, verbose way of saying that Daisy Miller had been in love with Frederick Winterbourne! This realization troubles Winterbourne, who makes no response to his aunt's question, for if it is true that Daisy had loved him, then it is also true that he had completely misunderstood her actions and had by his final rejection of her in some way hastened her death. In his final remark Winterbourne shows further realization of how his stiffened moral responses had violated both himself and another human being: " 'You were right in that remark that you made last summer. I was booked to make a mistake. I have lived too long in foreign parts' " (206).

Winterbourne seems to embody a number of insights here. He shows, first of all, that he has been away from his native land too long to be able to respond properly to "the American tone." In echoing his aunt's remark, he also seems to reject her notion that mistakes are made through ignorance of social conventions. He realizes that his mistake was forced upon him by too great a *commitment* to social convention. He also suggests that he might be ready to reject his foreign address and his commitment to Europeanized American values. With what he has learned about himself and his violation of another human being, that would seem at least a dramatically logical outcome of his insight. And if *Daisy Miller* were a tragic work, then James might very well have shown him to act just so.

But *Daisy Miller,* in spite of its heroine's death, is not a tragedy. It has been comic throughout, especially with a narrative sensibility that constantly points out the foibles of all the characters. And at the end it can be no less, showing the book's affinities with *Huckleberry Finn* and with the tradition of irony in Realistic fiction by bringing the book around in a final ironic circle. The last paragraph reads:

> Nevertheless, he went back to live at Geneva, whence there continue to come the most contradictory accounts of his motives of sojourn: a report that he is "studying" hard — an intimation that he is much interested in a very clever foreign lady. [207]

The reader is brought right back to the situation that obtained at the beginning of the story. Winterbourne is back where he started, perhaps better for his realizations but no different in his life style or circumstances. In short, Winterbourne's insight into himself has brought about no change in his life. But this outcome is to be expected, for most lives outside of books show few dramatic changes in circumstance, no matter how shattering the insight into self might be. Winterbourne returns to the bosom of his society because it is easy and comfortable to do so. Even though he knows in some part of his consciousness that following the rules, playing the game, has cost him most of his ability to make moral distinctions and choices and that he has, because of this capitulation, violated another human being, he nonetheless returns to the way of life that gives him the most security because it absolves him from the terrible burden of freedom.

James knows what Twain knows — that one cannot commit oneself completely to the workings of society without finally being violated as an individual and without violating others. And yet, it is not possible to exist outside of the social octopus, whose tentacles reach everywhere both to strangle and to soothe — in either way choking the life out of the self. Daisy's rebellion does her no good because she focuses it on a ubiquitous, undefeatable enemy and thereby destroys herself. Winterbourne's new consciousness is wasted because he is not strong enough to use it to change his life. There is no recourse in the conflict of self and society but to resign oneself to violation. Beyond this point the insights of Realism were not to go. Naturalism is merely a transmutation of this basic insight.

6

FROM REALISM TO NATURALISM

Realism is primarily a literary method; Naturalism is a way of interpreting the world. These statements seem self-evident, even hackneyed, but I stress them because the distinctions between Realism and Naturalism are quite complex. I emphasize the differences between the two terms while at the same time stressing that the novels that project the world view termed Naturalistic invariably use the literary method of Realism. It is not, of course, possible to draw sharp demarcations between method and vision, style and content. Literary methods always reflect a point of view, and the point of view, the sense of the world that each author (and every human being) carries somewhere inside his consciousness, manifests itself as much in the way a writer creates his fictional world as in what he has to say directly about that world.

The insights of the later Thoreau, of Melville, and of Hawthorne lead to the methods of Twain and James. A point of view that insists on stripping away both the world's superfluities and the preconceptions of the reader's consciousness leads finally to the position that the only way to experience value is to confront the naked self with the naked object. It further suggests that man's experiences of reality are constantly subject to the dangers of illusion because of his perceptual and cognitive preconceptions. But all three of the above writers still use an "old-fashioned" rhetoric that is tinged with echoes of the "Transcendentalist" style. What makes Twain so "modern" is

129

that he formed his style during a time when the new *ideas* manifest in the writings of Melville and Hawthorne had taken hold, and his style reflects the new commitment to omit the superfluous. Twain uses a stripped-down rhetoric that reduces imagery and metaphor, with almost no overt statements of value and with a largely indirect use of symbolism that is certainly not the "subject" of the book as it seems to be in *Moby-Dick* and *The Scarlet Letter*.

As in all the stages of Romanticism, Twain's Realism leads not only to its own downfall, but also into a new orientation that grows out of the old. The Realist ethic basically condemns man to the constant experience of nothingness as the price he pays for the pure value of direct confrontation. This attitude is certainly heroic, but it leads in at least two ways to the consistent violation of the self. The individual who has achieved a freedom of vision still finds it impossible to escape the mediating vision of a society that he may not accept but that everyone else does; and the individual may cease to believe in a world constituted by God, but he is then left with a world that depends for its existence only on the fallible human will. The situation is like building castles above an infinite abyss. Facing the world without a mediating vision may be intellectually possible, but when man faces reality with a belief in nothing but his own consciousness, he soon comes to believe that the world is a place of negative value. If Satan is the obverse of God, then the vision of the Naturalists is the other side of what the Transcendentalists insisted on finding in the world. It is not possible to believe for long in one's own insignificance before one comes to believe that the cards of the world are stacked against him.

The Red Badge of Courage: Between Realism and Naturalism

The Red Badge of Courage, although not quite a purely "Naturalistic" novel, nonetheless demonstrates the transition from Realism to Naturalism as well as any American book. Through the instrument of the Realistic style the author presents a vision of man as a creature his existence in and meaningful interaction with the world. The Naturalistic novel increasingly sees the individual consciousness, not as whose reality stems more from his primitive consciousness than from interacting with a society, but as swept along by the inchoate forces that control both the social order in which he is a citizen and the cosmic order in which he is a cipher. The *Red Badge of Courage* sees man as a physiological mote swept willy-nilly by the winds of circumstance.

Stephen Crane's semicomic Everyman, Henry Fleming, is an intentionally unheroic, undistinguished individual, who lacks the social standing of either Captain Ahab or Reverend Dimmesdale and the intuitive moral vision of Huckleberry Finn. He exists on a primitive level of consciousness in which his rationalizations — his distinguishing psychological characteristic — are a direct indication of his limited moral sense, rather than a comic device, as in *Huck Finn*. As an individual, Henry is nothing at all, a cipher of no significance who may be struck down at any moment by a bullet or a rifle butt; and as a social being he is a lowly private, without any standing whatever in the military hierarchy. Throughout most of the book he is nameless, called by his author "the youth," just as his companion Wilson is "the friend." By reducing Henry Fleming to namelessness, Crane denigrates him to the level of a simple consciousness who, in the midst of circumstances that sweep him away, rationalizes all his contradictory actions with continuous illogic.

Crane has been described as a literary impressionist who tries with verbal pigmentation to create the impression of a landscape emerging through hazy light. But this is merely a technique which embodies a much deeper urge in his writing. Here is the opening paragraph of the novel:

> The cold passed reluctantly from the earth, and the retiring fogs revealed an army stretched out on the hills, resting. As the landscape changed from brown to green, the army awakened, and began to tremble with eagerness at the noise of rumors. It cast its eyes upon the roads, which were growing from long troughs of liquid mud to proper thoroughfares. A river, amber-tinted in the shadow of its banks, purled at the army's feet; and at night, when the stream had become of a sorrowful blackness, one could see across it the red, eyelike gleam of hostile camp-fires set in the low brows of distant hills. [11][1]

1. Stephen Crane, *The Red Badge of Courage and other Stories,* ed. and introd. R. W. Stallman (New York: Signet, 1960). This edition collates all the editions Crane saw through the press as well as his manuscripts. All references appear in the text. Ordinarily I would not use a paperback edition as my text, but Stallman's work represents at present the definitive version of *The Red Badge of Courage*

By personifying the landscape with an almost mystic quality of emergence, especially when his human characters are emerging from sleep into consciousness, Crane attempts to embody a world that seethes with energies beyond man's control. He does not try to show a spiritual correspondence between man and nature in the manner of Transcendentalism; Crane creates a world that is full of its own kind of life and men that are full of theirs, though the two kinds of energies cannot possibly work together.

In Henry Fleming's universe the old traditions no longer obtain. Although in the beginning Henry sees the great war with the eyes of a boy —

> He had, of course, dreamed of battles all his life — of vague and bloody conflicts that had thrilled him with their sweep and fire. In visions he had seen himself in many struggles. [13]

— in his sober, more rational moments he understands that these youthful fantasies are no longer valid:

> From his home his youthful eyes had looked upon the war in his own country with distrust. It must be some sort of a play affair. He had long despaired of witnessing a Greeklike struggle. Such would be no more, he had said. Men were better, or more timid. Secular and religious education had effaced the throat-grappling instinct, or else firm finance held in check the passions. [13]

His reasoning follows a curiously contradictory line of thought that brings together both biological and economic determinism. For Crane, men's choices are determined by a combination of animal instincts and social institutions.

The society to which Henry submits himself — that of an army at war — is a hierarchy in which he has no function other than to obey orders. The private is asked to live on a minimal level of consciousness and moral responsibility, subject to the control of others and to forces that are larger than anything he could possibly be conscious of fighting for. There are no issues at stake in the war that Crane recreates in *The Red Badge;* there is only movement, frustration, and death. At night Union and Confederate soldiers talk to one another when on guard, but during the day the same people kill one another, because that is the way one behaves in wartime; they shoot when shot

---

(and will remain so until the relevant volume appears in the University of Virginia Edition of *The Work of Stephen Crane*).

at, they run when frightened, they are heroic by accident, and they are cowardly in the same way. Crane presents scene, action, and character through a highly controlled point of view that allows almost no authorial comment and judgment, a style that corresponds in its cold objectivity to the world in which the characters find themselves.

Because value exists in neither society nor situation, and because Crane posits nothing transcendent except natural energies, the only source of human identity lies within the individual consciousness. But this consciousness is not an autonomous unit that reflects either a consistent moral system or a coherent point of view. It reacts to situations, and the judgments it passes on its own actions are nothing more than rationalizations. However, rationalizations are a necessary defense. The environment is a continuous threat to the very existence of every human being, and because the individual can locate no value outside himself, he finds it humanly necessary to justify all he does by its role in perpetuating his sense of identity. When Henry runs, he composes in his head the following justification:

> He had fled, he told himself, because annihilation approached. He had done a good part in saving himself, who was a little piece of the army. He had considered the time, he said, to be one in which it was the duty of every little piece to rescue itself if possible. Later the officers could fit the little pieces together again, and make a battle front. If none of the little pieces were wise enough to save themselves from the flurry of death at such a time, why, then, where would be the army? It was all plain that he had proceeded according to very correct and commendable rules. His actions had been sagacious things. They had been full of strategy. They were the work of a master's legs. [51]

The substitution of "legs" for the expected "mind" is a clever ironic touch. But except for that, Crane lets Henry's rationalizations speak without any comment by the author; for Henry's rationalizations are his only source of personal value.

Crane as an incipient Naturalist sees two primary causes for human action: an external force — nameless, inchoate, but fully felt as a presence even if but partially understood — that sweeps the individual along its inexorable path; and the unconscious reactions that control most of the individual's responses and all his rationalizations, but which are themselves almost completely controlled by the external forces. When Henry experiences his first battle,

> He was bewildered. As he ran with his comrades he strenuously

> tried to think, but all he knew was that if he fell down those coming
> behind would tread upon him. All his faculties seemed to be needed to
> guide him over and past obstructions. He felt carried along by a mob.
> [30]

He does not choose his reactions; he simply becomes part of a mob
that has an individual will but no room for the responses of individuals.
He feels that the "iron laws of tradition and law" are closing in on him,
and when he later begins to fire his weapon, he feels this unspoken
force determining all his actions:

> He suddenly lost concern for himself, and forgot to look at a
> menacing fate. He became not a man but a member. He felt that some-
> thing of which he was a part — a regiment, an army, a cause, or a coun-
> try — was in a crisis. He was welded into a common personality which
> was dominated by a single desire. For some moments he could not flee
> no more than a little finger can commit a revolution from a hand. [41]

He tries to define the "something" that controls his actions, and he uses
a number of different words to isolate it; but he can know only how he
responds to that "something" because it is, in truth, indefinable.

The image of the finger on the hand completes the metaphor begun earlier when he felt "not a man but a member." Still later, when
he is trying to find his way back to his regiment, he attempts to state
his feelings of impotence more philosophically:

> He searched about in his mind for an adequate malediction for the
> indefinite cause, the thing upon which men turn the words of final blame.
> It — whatever it was — was responsible for him, he said. There lay the
> fault. [68]

There has always been something comic in blaming the stars rather
than ourselves for our failings, but I think that Crane takes Henry's
torment with some seriousness. When one has ceased to believe in a
source of value outside the self, it is still difficult to believe that blame
should be placed inside, especially when it is unclear whether or not
such blame is deserved. Henry's alternatives are so limited by his situation that the idea of moral praise or castigation is quite irrelevant.
In such situations moral values become, as Emerson noted in "Self-
Reliance," merely names.

Early in the book, when Henry discusses whether or not he will
run in battle, he unintentionally insults his companion. When the loud
soldier leaves indignantly, Henry feels "alone in space" like "a mental

outcast." He stretches out on his blanket and "In the darkness he saw visions of a thousand-tongued fear that would babble at his back and cause him to flee, while others were going coolly about their country's business" (27). And it is, of course, fear that causes him to run during his first action — fear and the mob psychology that causes everyone else to panic at the same time. He yells "with fright" and becomes as disoriented as a "proverbial chicken"; then he runs. And yet the fear that turns him irrational is no different from the emotion he feels later on when his acts are "heroic."

> Within him, as he hurled himself forward, was born a love, a despairing fondness for this flag which was near him. It was a creation of beauty and invulnerability. It was a goddess, radiant, that bended its form with an imperious gesture to him. It was a woman, red and white, hating and loving, that called him with the voice of his hopes. Because no harm could come to it he endowed it with power. He kept near, as if it could be a saver of lives, and an imploring cry went from his mind. [110]

His irrational flood of emotions — now that the momentum of battle is going his way — can be turned into an outward act of bravery rather than an inward panic; but they are two sides of the same emotion. Circumstance determines action.

Throughout everything the natural world is personified as permanent and indifferent:

> As he gazed around him the youth felt a flash of astonishment at the blue, pure sky and the sun-gleamings on the trees and fields. It was surprising that Nature had gone tranquilly on with her golden process in the midst of so much devilment. [45]

Nature, although she has her own life force, is not involved with the lives of men, except indirectly. Even at the end of the book when Henry has achieved a false sense of equanimity Crane once more emphasizes nature's indifference:

> But the sky would forget. It was true, he admitted, that in the world it was the habit to cry devil at persons who refused to trust what they could not trust, but he thought that perhaps the stars dealt differently. The imperturbable sun shines on insult and worship. [132]

Man cannot turn to the stars for solace, and his attempts to blame the universe for his plight are comic.

But an even more pointed key to Crane's attitudes can be found in his imagery. Consistent with the view of man projected by such Darwinists as Spencer and Huxley, Crane's imagery presents man as an animal subject paradoxically to mechanical forces. It is worth tracing this imagery to see how the strange combination of metaphors operates and to watch the use of imagery undergo a shift as the fate of Henry Fleming begins to change.

"They were going to look at war, the red animal — war, the blood-swollen god" (32). War, the animal-like god that is variously described as a monster and a dragon, is liable to swallow the smaller human animals who hunt in its territory. When the regiment is faring badly, "The colonel, perchance to relieve his feelings, began to scold like a wet parrot" (40). And when Henry first experiences the confusion and terror of battle, "He developed the acute exasperation of a pestered animal, a well-meaning cow worried by dogs" (42). He begins to feel like a "driven beast." Shortly before he runs, he feels even greater terror: "Into the youth's eyes there came a look that one can see in the orbs of a jaded horse" (47). He finally runs "like a rabbit" (47). After running and ending up with the wounded when he has no real wound of his own, he feels like "a worm" (69), "a craven loon" (70), a "moth" (70). He rationalizes by saying that at certain times even "men of courage . . . scurry like chickens" (70–71). " 'Good Gawd,' the youth grumbles, 'we're always being chased around like rats!' " (96). He becomes like a hunted animal, "a kitten chased by boys" (98), and he sets his teeth "in a curlike snarl" (98). "The tormentors were flies sucking insolently at his blood" (98). Such quotations could be multiplied indefinitely.

When matters begin to go better for the regiment, however, the imagery changes. Wilson says, " 'Th' boys fight like hell-roosters' " (94). The lieutenant crows to Henry, " 'By heavens, if I had ten thousand wild cats like you I could tear th' stomach outa this war in less'n a week!' " (100). The men begin to fight well. "They huddled no more like sheep" (108). Henry notes "the vicious, wolflike temper of his comrades" (114). By the time the tide of battle has really swung toward a Union victory, "They launched themselves as at the throats of those who stood resisting" (127). When Henry sees the flag of the enemy regiment, "He plunged like a mad horse at it" (127). The shift in the imagery is obvious.

In his continuous metaphor Crane suggests that under the wrong circumstances men will behave like weak animals, under the right ones like strong ones. But men are always animals, and the mere fact that they have a more sophisticated consciousness than dogs and horses does not change the fact that in a universe totally indifferent to human beings an individual can demand nothing more than to be at the arbitrary whim of fate and circumstance. The movement from Emerson's vision seems almost complete.

The other half of Crane's world view envisions a mechanistic universe that runs continuously with the animal metaphor. Men at war are cogs in a great machine. When Henry watches the gunners fire enthusiastically at the enemy while he himself is running, he thinks of them as "Methodical idiots! Machinelike fools!" (49). And when his panic is over, he becomes curious once more about the state of the battle:

> Presently he proceeded again on his forward way. The battle was like the grinding of an immense and terrible machine to him. Its complexities and powers, its grim processes, fascinated him. He must go close and see it produce corpses. [56]

This view of the war as an immense machine that produces commodities continues in his feelings about the Union army:

> His education had been that success for that mighty blue machine was certain; that it would make victories as a contrivance turns out buttons. [72]

Later, when things go less well for a moment, he thinks that "the regiment was a machine run down" (112). Still later, when the battle begins to go better for his side, the martial sounds take on cosmic connotations:

> To those in the midst of it it became a din fitted to the universe. It was the whirring and thumping of gigantic machinery, complications among the smaller stars. [122]

The universal war machine obeys the laws of mechanics. Once again the images can be multiplied.

This concatenated imagery presents two major impulses of what have come to be called Naturalism; man as animal and the universe as machine. These ideas develop side by side throughout the book, giving the impression that mechanical laws govern a biological world in which not necessarily the fittest, but certainly the luckiest, survive. Both the laws of the universe and the interests of man are autonomous, and although both exist in the same space-time, they do not interact with reciprocity. Neither the universe nor the individual has any signficance; they just are.

Henry Fleming seems in some way to have learned that Naturalistic lesson. The reader is told that "He had been to touch the great death, and found that, after all, it was but the great death" (134). If one believes that man's life has no cosmic significance, that man is not here for any purpose other than to exist in a meaningless universe, then death is no longer the great mystery, for it opens up nothing on the other side. Not even as mysterious as Ahab's "pasteboard mask," it is just that event that lies at the end of the future. But some caution must be applied to the conclusions Henry draws about himself. Throughout *The Red Badge* he rationalizes every one of his actions, showing thereby that the human capacity for self-justification is unlimited. And now, at the end of the book we are told:

> He had been an animal blistered and sweating in the heat and pain of war. He turned now with a lover's thirst to images of tranquil skies, fresh meadows, cool brooks — an existence of soft and eternal peace.
> Over the river a golden ray of sun came through the hosts of leaden rain clouds. [134]

Taken at face value, these words are too idyllic to fit credibly with the rest of the book. Crane shows Henry making a final ironic rationalization in order to complete the cycle of his self-delusion. Perhaps he has achieved a certain humility, but he has certainly not become "a man" in so short a time. Who knows how he will respond in the next battle? Even more, what difference does it make? He could be struck down by an arbitrary bullet the following day, and all his moral transformation would mean exactly nothing in any context larger than that of his own life — which is all that it has meant anyway. What solidifies this reading of the end of the book is the last sentence, which is given a place all by itself. It is the kind of easy emotion common in cheap fiction and the movies, in which moral transformations always seem to be symbolized by sudden changes in the weather. But cheap emotion has been a subject of irony throughout *The Red Badge*. There are no easy transformations. Crane has stated only two pages earlier that "The imperturbable sun shines on insult and worship" (132), stressing, as always, the permanence and indifference of nature. To present a sun that suddenly smiles with meaning on Henry Fleming at the end of the book would be to violate everything that has gone before. The last lines must be read ironically if the reader is to continue to take the book with final seriousness on its own terms. Man remains an insignificant creature at the whim of forces in a universe he cannot control; and in reaction to uncontrollable circumstances he can do nothing more than rationalize.

Stephen Crane, although viscerally deterministic, is not a Naturalist in the full sense of Jack London, Frank Norris, and Theodore Dreiser. These writers believed in an *ideology* of determinism that grew out of their various readings in Marx, Darwin, Huxley, Spencer, Zola, and Nietzsche, mixed with temperaments that no doubt found these thinkers' ideas congenial. Crane, however, seems to have come upon his deterministic world view largely through his direct response to the world, examined without a mediating vision in the classic Realist manner. He dramatizes man's lack of free will without simply trying to demonstrate it as a philosophical point, and the lesson of Henry Fleming is thus more vivid than that, say, of one of Jack London's dogs. This is not to say that all Naturalistic fiction is merely thesis-ridden. The best of it, such as *Sister Carrie*, does transcend its ideology to present characters with experiences just as vivid as Henry Fleming's. And it is, after all, just this dramatic vividness of experience that constitutes much of what is considered valuable in fiction.

Sister Carrie and the Sentimentality of Nihilism

Sister Carrie is the first major American work of what I would call pure Naturalism, and it is in many ways still the best. In it, Dreiser displays an observant understanding of the underbelly of American society that is rare in our fiction, and he creates a set of unforgettable characters and a form that, in spite of the often dreadful "writing," seems somehow to balance perfectly the various parts of the book.

Dreiser is a full-fledged Naturalist in ways that Crane was not. His distinctly ideological point of view is most immediately reflected in the chapter titles to *Sister Carrie*. The first title, "A Waif Amid Forces," for instance, explains the "message" of the book with embarrassing baldness, for as Carrie turns this way and that in her tortured climb up the ladder, it becomes clear that she is never really free to choose the road to her own happiness. Bound by the predetermined circumstances of her background, her environment, and the men she is with, she is a waif amid the forces of the universe that determine each man's fate. Dreiser is always so anxious to make his ideological point that he will step directly into the tale at any time to say what he thinks. It would be fatuous to condemn this characteristic out of hand, however, since, as Wayne Booth has shown, it is only a modernist prejudice, after James, to insist that authorial comments are illegitimate and that a novel must make all its effects "dramatically."[1]

Even so, the great moments in *Sister Carrie* are not those that automatically confirm the author's stated philosophy or those in which the intrusive author makes a long philosophical point; they are, rather, those moments in which an event does confirm the author's point of view dramatically, as during the scene in which Hurstwood removes the money from the safe.

To deal with *Sister Carrie* as a work of Naturalism, the focus must be on the interaction between Dreiser's comments and his dramatic presentation of character and situation; this will reveal whether his fictional presentation does coordinate with his ideological predispositions. The two strains do run closely together and, aside from some poorly written passages, there is no conflict between them. The opening chapter of the book is a microcosm of the whole.

Dreiser seems quite aware at all times of describing a sociohistorical phenomenon. In the first chapter he explains the lure of the city ("The Magnet Attracting") on a girl ("A Waif Amid Forces") from a small country town. For Dreiser the true reality of modern life is a city like Chicago, whose allure goes beyond anything man can control. He makes this clear in the novel's third paragraph, the first half of which explicitly sets the theme of both the chapter and the book:

> When a girl leaves her home at eighteen, she does one of two things. Either she falls into saving hands and becomes better, or she rapidly assumes the cosmopolitan standard of virtue and becomes worse. Of an intermediate balance, under the circumstances, there is no possibility. The city has its cunning wiles, no less than the infinitely smaller and more human tempter. There are large forces which allure with all the soulfulness of expression possible in the most cultured human. The

1. Wayne Booth, *The Rhetoric of Fiction* (Chicago: University of Chicago Press, 1961), pp. 50–53.

gleam of a thousand lights is often as effective as the persuasive light in a wooing and fascinating eye. Half the undoing of the unsophisticated and natural mind is accomplished by forces wholly superhuman. [5-6][2]

Dreiser sees the moral possibilities of contemporary urban life as subject to certain absolute alternatives — not choices. Once a girl gets to the city, she will either "fall" into some kind of salvation or sink into the immoral morass. The city is like a seething ocean, with "cunning wiles" and "large forces" that are "wholly superhuman," where one survives or dies largely as a result of circumstances. Even Crane, who presents the situation of war so as to suggest forces beyond man's control, does not insist *as a philosophical postulate* that man is in a situation wholly predetermined and beyond his control.

Dreiser's method of characterization is to give an outline before presenting his character dramatically. Before he describes the physical presence of Carrie, he tells the reader that "She was eighteen years of age, bright, timid, and full of the illusions of ignorance and youth" (5). Dreiser is fond of such cataloguing statements. It is as though he feels that by accumulating enough of them, he can give a complete sense of what makes his character tick. In many ways this attitude is a substitute for his lack of the persistent analytic insight of *The Red Badge of Courage,* for *Sister Carrie* is that strange kind of book in which the reader feels he knows all there is to know about how a character behaves and yet finds that he knows almost nothing about the unconscious dimensions of his mind. Dreiser continues to catalogue Carrie's visible traits: "Self-interest with her was high but not strong" (6); "she was a fair example of the middle American class — two generations removed from the emigrant" (6); "And yet she was interested in her charms, quick to understand the keener pleasures of life, ambitious to gain in material things" (6). Statements such as these, along with many others, serve to present Carrie almost completely through external details and her sociohistorical characteristics.

Dreiser handles Charles Drouet in the same manner, presenting him by a catalogue of characteristics and treating him more like a social phenomenon than like a person. With his unerring eye for the surface, Dreiser does not miss a single aspect of his clothing, for in-

2. Theodore Dreiser, *Sister Carrie,* ed. and introd. Claude Simpson (Boston: Houghton Mifflin, 1959; this reproduces the first edition of 1900). All references appear in the text.

stance, that would be necessary to characterize him as a "drummer," from his flashy suit to the high polish of his shoes. Having already characterized Carrie as the kind of person who is "ambitious to gain in material things," Dreiser can then describe the interaction of the two people as a logical outcome of his catalogue of their characteristics. He writes of Drouet: "He was, for the order of intellect represented, attractive, and whatever he had to recommend him, you may be sure was not lost upon Carrie, in this, her first glance" (7).

After describing the drummer as a social type, "lest this order of individual should permanently pass," Dreiser presents the interaction of the two passengers, noting after a while that "there was much more passing now than the mere words indicated" (9). One would expect at this point that he might dramatize in some way the unconscious flow of feelings he suggests, but the next two lines are somewhat abstract: "He recognized the indescribable thing that made up for fascination and beauty in her. She realized that she was of interest to him from the one standpoint which a woman both delights in and fears." This kind of indirection and euphemism hardly dramatizes feelings or indicates a great deal more "than the mere words indicated." He speaks *about* the feelings that lie beneath the surface without presenting them directly and thus gives the impression that the character's depths have been plumbed when in reality they have only been mentioned. Dreiser nevertheless shows that a careful examination of the surface and at least a recognition of something underneath is one possible mode of convincing characterization. A page later Dreiser shows how the two characters he has catalogued for us interact and drift together without realizing it. Once again he stays on the surface, recognizing the existence of unconscious motivations but not presenting them:

> How true it is that words are but the vague shadows of the volumes we mean. Little audible links, they are, chaining together great inaudible feelings and purposes. Here were these two, bandying little phrases, drawing purses, looking at cards, and both unconscious of how inarticulate all their real feelings were. Neither was wise enough to be sure of the working of the mind of the other. He could not tell how his luring succeeded. She could not realise that she was drifting, until he secured her address. Now she felt that she had yielded something — he, that he had gained a victory. Already they felt that they were somehow associated. Already he took control in directing the conversation. His words were easy. Her manner was relaxed. [10-11]

Is Dreiser uncommunicative about the unconscious because his characters themselves are so inarticulate? Does this sufficiently justify his staying on the surface? I think not, especially considering the character of Henry Fleming, surely a person of no higher social standing than Carrie and even less than Drouet. But Crane seems able to present all the conflicts that torment Henry, as well as all his mental processes. At the root of the contrast is Dreiser's conception of what constitutes the reality of mental processes, which is quite different from Crane's. If Crane feels that man's fate is so determined by circumstance that his mind becomes a silly victim of the need for rationalization, then Dreiser feels man's lack of free will is so strong that his suppression by "forces" is the only reality that matters and that what goes on inside his head is insignificant beside the buffeting of fate. For this reason his characters drift into situations and are not given choices. And for this reason Dreiser sets up his characters almost as geometric postulates, representing social and personality types much in the manner of Gertrude Stein (for example, in *Three Lives* and *The Making of Americans*). Given the qualities of their consciousnesses and their social situations, his characters must react in the way Dreiser describes. Drouet, because he is a "drummer," cannot help trying to seduce young ladies. And Carrie, being a young girl off the farm, cannot help responding. They act and react without choosing; they drift.

This seems to be Dreiser's view of human relationships. The self never draws nourishment from within. It can feed only by drawing on its position in society, its good fortune in finding situations, its ability to deal with drives on the inside and forces on the outside, and the way in which — without quite knowing why — it can interact with other human beings whose selves define themselves in quite the same way. There are weak types and strong types, and when these types come together, the reaction is predictable. What is interesting to note is how, at the end of a century-long Romantic tradition, the individual comes to see himself once again as a helpless victim of fate in much the same way the Negative Romantics did; but the sources of this feeling are much different.

The Negative Romantic experienced psychic and cosmic dislocation because for him the world order that had sustained man for centuries had broken down. Through a belief in the deity of organized religion or the deity of reason, society had always had a transcendent sanction and, through this sanction, so had the individual self. But when this base collapsed, so did the individual's belief in his own selfhood and in the possibility of achieving a meaningful society.

The Naturalistic vision that arises in American literature at the end of the century — at least thirty years later than, say, in France — emerges after a long dialectic in which many different orientations attempt to solve the problems first discovered by such Negative Romantics as Poe; and it is felt first by writers who were born after the Civil War, the point in our history that unalterably ushered in the new urban-industrial civilization. But Drieser's characters' disorientation is not based on the collapse of order. On the contrary, his characters feel alienated because of the overwhelming presence of so much order that they cannot even conceive of understanding or controlling it. The Naturalistic vision was an inevitable outgrowth of a metaphysic that postulated as the only source of value the direct, unmediated confrontation of naked subject and naked object. Dreiser is the clearest and most consistent manifestation of the new vision in American literature precisely because in him this vision has an ideological base and in his fictional presentation this ideology is dramatized consistently in his characters' lives.

For Dreiser the self is violated by simply existing in a world whose arbitrary meaninglessness is made more evident by the very fact that man can live and survive in it without a transcendent belief in anything, even his own will, and without even the value that Crane gives to the powers of rationalization. At least, Crane seems to say, if a man cannot discover value in the world, he can delude himself. But Dreiser does not even allow Carrie or Hurstwood to maintain any illusions. Only Drouet in the end seems firmly ensconced in his false visions; but Dreiser has long since dismissed him as a character of any importance. In fact, Dreiser constantly makes it clear that illusions must be destroyed; not because a clear head is necessary if the individual is to lead a moral life, but because the pull of reality is for any conscious individual much stronger than the world of his fantasies, and sooner or later it cannot be denied. On the approach to Chicago, Carrie looks out of the window and is captivated by the sight of the huge industrial metropolis. As the author puts it, "To the child, the genius with imagination, or the wholly untravelled, the approach to a great city for the first time is a wonderful thing" (11). This is not just the sentimental expression of a Wordsworthian child cultist; Dreiser prepares the reader with those phrases for what happens when Carrie meets her sister:

> Carrie realised the change of affectional atmosphere at once. Amid all the maze, uproar, and novelty she felt cold reality taking her by the hand. No world of light and merriment. No round of amusement. Her sister carried with her most of the grimness of shift and toil. [12]

Whether one likes it or not, dreams and illusions are the nearest most people can come to the old belief in the transcendent. But in Dreiser this kind of empty Transcendentalism is quickly dashed by the cold water of reality that does not permit the conscious individual to live in his illusions for long.

Dreiser ends the opening chapter with the following image of Carrie: "With her sister she was much alone, a lone figure in a tossing, thoughtless sea" (13). Once again he harks back to a traditional nineteenth-century figure — the individual as a solitary figure tossed on the waves like Rimbaud's drunken boat. Dreiser emphasizes the individual's solitary alienation amid the teeming life of a city composed of endless forms of energy. The sea of modern life is "thoughtless," not because it is inconsiderate, but because it simply gives no thought to the individual, lacking the consciousness to do so. The energies of the modern world have all the structures found in human beings except the structures of the mind. To think teleologically about the life of urban-industrial America is an absurdity. Life simply has no purpose, and because of this it is inimical to man — but not consciously or actively so. Man's life seems inimical because it is not possible for him to exist without thinking that there is some purpose to his existence and thus to existence as a whole. And yet such satisfaction is an impossibility.

Though by and large the narrative's dramatic unfolding bears out this bleak vision, Dreiser himself contradicts it on a number of occasions, and these contradictions are one of the interesting sources of tension in Dreiser's vision of man. Chapter VIII, "Intimations by Winter: An Ambassador Summoned," begins with a long philosophical paragraph in which the author presents his doctrine of man's lack of free will and, combining it with popular evolutionary theory, arrives at a strange vision of transcendence. The paragraph opens with images of Naturalistic determinism before moving immediately to images taken from the great chain of being:

> Among the forces which sweep and play throughout the universe, untutored man is but a wisp in the wind. Our civilisation is still in a middle stage, scarcely beast, in that it is no longer wholly guided by instinct; scarcely human, in that it is not yet wholly guided by reason. [67]

Dreiser seems to be combining his own deeply felt, although scarcely original, feelings about the universe with the popular conundrum that reason lies at the ideal end of human development. He compares man with the tiger on whom "no responsibility rests" because, as an animal in the jungle, the tiger is "aligned by nature with the forces of life," and since he is "without thought he is protected." Dreiser locates man on the evolutionary scale, but he combines the moralistic overtones of the medival great chain with the terminology of Naturalism: "As a beast, the forces of life aligned him with them; as a man, he has not yet wholly learned to align himself with the forces." The exact position of man's "isthmus of a middle state" (to use Pope's phrase) is determined by his relationship to the universal "forces" with which a man must learn "to align himself." The only problem with these suggestions is that Dreiser himself makes it clear throughout the book that aligning oneself with universal forces assures one of nothing. It can be done, not through an act of the will, but only through acquiescence. Even more, there is no assurance, first of all, that these forces can be known, and second, that successful acquiescence can assure the satisfaction of inner needs. Carrie is a good example of this view.

What I find most fascinating about this passage, however, are the concluding lines that introduce Dreiser's feelings of transcendence into a context where they simply do not fit:

> We have the consolation of knowing that evolution is ever in action, that the ideal is a light that cannot fail. He will not forever balance thus between good and evil. When this jangle of free-will and instinct shall have been adjusted, when perfect understanding has given the former the power to replace the latter entirely, man will no longer vary. The needle of understanding will yet point steadfast and unwavering to the distant pole of truth. [67–68]

Dreiser postulates a universe in which all elements coalesce into a unity, with a single transcendent point toward which everything tends.

This attitude, so strongly at variance with images presented elsewhere in the novel, can only mean that deep in Dreiser and in many of the so-called Naturalists, such as Frank Norris, there was a yearning for transcendence that increased steadily as their visions of a meaningless universe overwhelmed them. In part of his moral consciousness Dreiser is not ready to exist in a world that is beyond good and evil; but that is unfortunately the kind of world his sensibility inhabits.

In this lies the novel's key philosophical tension. On one side is the sense that the individual can do nothing but submit to "forces," and on the other is the hope that, in the broadest terms, evolution has the transcendent goal of "truth." This kind of vague yearning is one reason for my calling Dreiser's Nihilism sentimental. However, the sentimental Transcendentalism evident here and elsewhere in the book is so obviously grafted on that it does not vitiate the central thrust of the narrative. In *The Octopus,* for instance, the energies that thrust through the waving wheat become a kind of pseudo-mystical animism that blurs the focus of Norris's narrative and ultimately becomes a way to avoid the harsher implications of his vision.

More consistent with his Naturalism, Dreiser sees that moral distinctions arise primarily out of instincts. Man's higher faculties do not begin in a dignified and rational moral sense; they arise from the roots of human consciousness:

> For all the liberal analysis of Spencer and our modern naturalistic philosophers, we have but an infantile perception of morals. There is more in the subject than mere conformity to a law of evolution. It is yet deeper than conformity to things of earth alone. It is more involved than we, as yet, perceive. Answer, first, why the heart thrills; explain wherefore some plaintive note goes wandering about the world, undying; make clear the rose's subtle alchemy evolving its ruddy lamp in light and rain. In the essence of these facts lie the first principles of morals. [81]

Dreiser always emphasizes man's relatedness to the animal and natural world. His metaphors are of fish in the sea, animal instincts, animated forces. His favorite sciences are those of evolution and physiological chemistry, and he invokes them as authorities whenever he can. Dreiser shares the positivistic view of the middle and late nineteenth century, which saw man in terms of measurable quantities; this vision of man as much as anything helped to depersonalize the individual sense of self. In describing Hurstwood's decline, Dreiser uses two scientific metaphors, one evolutionary and the other chemical. He speaks of the need to adapt to a specific environment, and he shows that a man is rarely conscious of the moment when the tide of his life begins to turn. Dreiser mentions Hurstwood's comfort with his money and his "rich" style of life. But he talks of money as though it had a life force of its own. "A fortune, like a man, is an organism which draws to itself other minds and other strength than that inherent in the founder" (274). Hurstwood's money clearly controls him more than he controls it. After describing the possible effects of money, Dreiser goes on to state that in his attachment to his fortune, the individual often loses consciousness of all other considerations:

> The man wanes, the need continues or grows, and the fortune, fallen into whose hands it may, continues. Hence, some men never recognise the turning in the tide of their abilities. It is only in chance cases, where a fortune or a state of success is wrested from them, that the lack of ability to do as they did formerly becomes apparent. Hurstwood, set down under new conditions, was in a position to see that he was no longer young. If he did not, it was due wholly to the fact that his state was so well balanced that an absolute change for the worse did not show. [274]

The change in a man's fortune (a term Dreiser seemingly uses to mean both luck and money) does not depend on what goes on inside him. As an organism, man is subject to the vagaries of circumstance and environment. When an organism changes its environment, it must adapt successfully. Hurstwood does not. He thrives in the warm seas of Chicago, where he has built a successful career on his knowledge of social behavior: how to dress, how to talk, how to ingratiate himself with his clientele. But the same manners do not work in New York, chiefly because Hurstwood does not have the money to buy the right kind of place, but also because he is not used to the New York style. He cannot adapt.

In the following paragraph Dreiser switches his metaphor, now performing a chemical analysis of the "katastates" and "anastates" produced in Hurstwood's blood by his depression. Once again Dreiser relies on a pseudo-scientific metaphor that forces the reader to see man as an organism subject to cold, objective laws rather than as a creature of moral consciousness and sensitivity.

But why does Carrie survive and even thrive, while Hurstwood moves steadily on "the road downward [which] has but few landings and level places"? For one, she is young enough not to be set in an unshakable life style. But in addition, Carrie's movement is primarily vertical, while Hurstwood's is horizontal. In terms of the social scale, Carrie climbs. She begins alone, in a setting that promises nothing more than a lifetime of the shabby but "moral" poverty that is her sister's lot. She is immediately attracted to Drouet, a man who on the surface has all the glitter of wealth. But as the months pass and Carrie's instincts develop into habits, she realizes that Drouet's appeal is primarily flashy, and she sees that the more subdued richness of Hurstwood has a higher social value. She drifts toward the latter and is eventually kidnapped by him. But like a cat, she always lands on her feet. Her social needs are not nearly as tied to pleasing the external world as are Hurstwood's, and she can therefore shift from one environment to another. Carrie's progression from man to man takes her steadily upward, from Drouet to Hurstwood to Ames. The change is always instinctive. Carrie drifts; she does not choose. But her instinctive drifting always takes her to the next higher step. It is not possible for a man to remain static, because to remain stationary, as Hurstwood does in New York, is eventually to begin to decline. A business that does not grow begins to lose ground almost immediately and will ultimately fail, and so, too, with an individual. Dreiser therefore sees vertical movement as the only possible mode of survival, for anyone who moves horizontally without a corresponding upward thrust, has already lost the game.

Once again, for Dreiser, drift is the major movement of the individual. It is the man who is shrewd either by instinct or by luck who can ride the drift in the proper direction. In the face of such a world view, all moral questions necessarily pale, because if the sole human problem becomes the right kind of instinctive drifting, then it hardly matters how someone lives his life. Society cannot be redeemed by the individual. It is not responsive to him in any way; in fact, in order even to survive, man must be responsive to the forces that drive *society*. Because choice is denied the individual, any moral action as traditionally defined is impossible. That is why Dreiser's tale can deviate so sanguinely from the conventional American standards of his time. Morality as his society defined it simply did not exist for him on any profound level.[3]

3. An interesting discussion of Dreiser's moral complexity is contained in Ellen Moers, *Two Dreisers* (New York: Viking, 1969). See also W. A. Swanberg,

It is because of Dreiser's dramatic instinct that he does not simply present the doctrine that choice is beyond man but can render this dilemma dramatically. I think particularly of the scene in which Hurstwood lifts the money from the safe and of the scene in *An American Tragedy* when Clyde Griffiths takes Roberta out on the lake to murder her. Dreiser establishes the first scene with exceeding dramatic care. All the central characters are undergoing extreme psychological disorientations. Drouet has just found out that Carrie has been seeing Hurstwood. He tells Carrie that Hurstwood is married, and because of this information Carrie refuses to see the manager, finally sending him a note that breaks off their relationship. In the process, however, she has had to insult Drouet past the point where they can stay together. Mrs. Hurstwood has discovered her husband's misbehavior, and their already impossible relationship is torn beyond stitching. She pressures Hurstwood, finally driving him out of the house, demanding money, and then going to her lawyer. And so, at the point when he is tempted by the open safe, Hurstwood has already lost Carrie, has been moved out of his house, and has been threatened with the scandal of a divorce that will finish him at Fitzgerald & Moy's. The tension for both character and reader is very high. The situation seems beyond solution, just as his situation does for Clyde Griffiths twenty-four years later.

That evening Hurstwood drinks more than usual to shake his depression, and with false elation he enters the office just before he closes the saloon. He tries the safe, and discovering it open, he takes out the money. Only the cashier and the owners know the combination. He holds the money and then puts it back. In the midst of this torture Dreiser philosophizes:

> We must remember that it may not be a knowledge of right, for no knowledge of right is predicated of the animal's instinctive recoil at evil. Men are still led by instinct before they are regulated by knowledge. It is instinct which recalls the criminal — it is instinct (where highly organised reasoning is absent) which gives the criminal his feeling of danger, his fear of wrong. [220]

Once again, it is "instinct," not "knowledge," that defines moral choice for Dreiser; and the moral choice is not the kind that is preached from the pulpit. By his discussion of instincts and by all

---

Dreiser (New York: Scribner, 1965), for a thorough documentation of Dreiser's almost heroic sexual life.

the mitigating circumstances with which he surrounds the scene Dreiser is trying to make clear that the line between right and wrong, preached from the pulpit By his discussion of instincts and by all good and evil, criminal and law-abiding citizens, is invisible. Hurstwood handles the money, he takes it out, puts it back, he takes it out again, and then somehow the door closes. "While the money was in his hand the lock clicked. It had sprung! Did he do it?" (222)

How does one assign criminality in such a situation? The safe door seems to have closed by itself, just as at the last minute, in *An American Tragedy,* Roberta drowns by accident in the lake. Hurstwood has not *committed* a crime. This would imply that he had made some kind of choice and acted upon it. No, he merely drifted into his situation. Moral or immoral actions simply happen. Nowhere else in the book does Dreiser dramatize so well the inability of an individual to commit any kind of action, to make any decision as to his destiny. A more analytically oriented writer might have insisted that Hurstwood's unconscious inclination was to take the money and that he therefore closed the door himself without even realizing it. But Dreiser barely hints at this possibility with the question, "Did he do it?" He prefers, as always, to leave the situation with the suggestion that the vague forces of circumstance have somehow conspired against the individual. And it is in this sense he has communicated throughout the novel. From the time the safe door is closed, the rest of Hurstwood's destiny is tightly sealed by an iron chain of necessity. Even his kidnapping of Carrie is an instinctive reaction, born of momentary necessity and of the situation into which blind fate has thrust him.

The view of man that Dreiser presents here and throughout his work is certainly a bleak one, but it follows necessarily from the orientation he inherits from previous writers and develops even further into a full-blown ideological Naturalism. Although Dreiser's Naturalism is a logical outgrowth of the Realist vision, his position leads him, not out of the Realist bind, but even further into a corner that he cannot escape without finally changing his basic assumptions about the world. Not only has Dreiser been unable to find even a partial solution to the need for a positive relationship between the individual and his society, he does not even solve the problem of protecting the individual from the inevitable violations of simply living. To face the world with neither free will nor protective illusion is to insist that life is no more than a steady series of unavoidable violations by other men, by society as a whole, and by the thoughtless universe.

But it is impossible to maintain such a vision without some kind of psychological modification. For this reason one feels in Dreiser the kind of tension I mentioned earlier — a tension between his belief in both rigid determinism and a sentimental Transcendentalism that has nothing to do with either religion or Emerson. Dreiser thrusts the latter upon his material because he finds it emotionally impossible not to see cosmic meaning even in a world so continuously reductive of human value. Throughout *Sister Carrie* it is clear that life is meaningless and that the individual cannot reenter society; and yet a sense of yearning also pervades the book — unconscious for the main part, but surfacing quite often — that something *has* to be done; in spite of what one knows.

At the end of the novel, after Dreiser has disposed of all the characters and shown the emptiness of their lives and hopes, Carrie sits in her famous rocking chair and looks out the window dreaming about the "ideal." Dreiser has made it copiously clear that happiness for her and for everyone else is an almost comic aspiration. Carrie can continue to rise higher and higher, conquering instinctively the sphere — the theater, where she can play roles — that she has fallen into almost by accident. But she will never satisfy her inner yearnings. And Dreiser will not allow her the illusion that she is happy, for that would be to violate his vision with a happy ending. Dreiser is guilty, however, as he is many times during the book, of a specious sentimentality in the midst of his Nihilism. Here is the final paragraph:

> Oh, Carrie, Carrie! Oh, blind strivings of the human heart! Onward, onward, it saith, and where beauty leads, there it follows. Whether it be the tinkle of a lone sheep bell o'er some quiet landscape, or the glimmer of beauty in sylvan places, or the show of soul in some passing eye, the heart knows and makes answer, following. It is when the feet weary and hope seems vain that the heartaches and the longings arise. Know, then, that for you is neither surfeit nor content. In your rocking-chair, by your window dreaming, shall you long, alone. In your rocking-chair, by your window, shall you dream such happiness as you may never feel. [418]

The language here is ersatz sublime; it is the kind of specious transcendence found in cheap fiction. Every line contains a resounding cliché that one can read only with pain. But it is obvious that

Dreiser's resources have been taxed past their limit by the vision of life he has presented in his narrative. As tough-minded as he is for the most part, he cannot bear to leave either Carrie or the reader without giving them an Arcadia to which they might aspire. The failure of Dreiser's Naturalism — and of almost all works in that mode — is the self-pity that seems to find its way between the lines of the bleak narrative; it is a necessary outgrowth of a vision that denies the significance of both man and his institutions. Not that the Naturalists were wrong in making this denial. Given the assumptions they inherited from a century of Romanticism, that was all they could see; and Dreiser's presentation of a world without meaning is so powerful that it cannot be easily refuted. But it is impossible to live with such a vision for long, and no one shows this more clearly than Dreiser himself in the yearning sentimentality of his Nihilism. The problem of the nineteenth century remains for the twentieth century to solve.

7

CONCLUSION

Naturalism did not solve the problems of the Realist orientation; it merely exacerbated them. As long as there is no way to believe in a mediating vision, as long as reality consists only of the phenomenal, then no teleology is conceivable, and individuals feel constantly violated by circumstance. There is still no rationale that can prevent one individual from violating another except by appealing to his sense of altruism; but no possible reason exists for altruism. Some way was needed of maintaining the toughness of the Realist vision while minimizing the violation of the individual personality. The grounds of disorientation had to be shifted away from the self. Something of this sort did happen in the next stage of culture — Stylism, more commonly called Aestheticism. The former word is preferable because style pervades all areas of life, not merely the so-called aesthetic. Style is the accepted pattern of behavior that each culture creates to handle certain categories of situations; but it is also the pattern of behavior that every person uses to deal with individual circumstances in order to bridge the gap between the cultural model and the disorienting facts of individual situations.

Stylism is often thought of in connection with a kind of *fin de siècle* malaise, a sense of ennui too enervating to be endured. But that is a misconception. The nineteenth-century dandy may seem effete, but his sense of style is his major key to maintaining integrity in the face of the most terrible kinds of alienation and within the realization that there is no place for an individual to remain unviolated and still live within the confines of society. His sense of style is what shields the individual from violation and at the same time allows him both to maintain an uncompromisng vision and to avoid falling into Naturalistic sentimentality. Personal style is what such individuals as Swinburne, Wilde, and, later, Hemingway used to symbolize the self; although the question still remained of how to *be* that self. This problem remains unsolved by Stylism, as does to a large extent the problem of reentering society, for the mark of the dandy is self-conscious alienation.

In the United States major work was not done in the Stylist mode until around 1900, beginning with the later style of Henry James and continuing with the work of Gertrude Stein, T. S. Eliot, Ezra Pound, Ernest Hemingway, Wallace Stevens, and William Faulkner, to name a few. All of these, however — certainly all those after James — found ways to transcend Stylism, largely by adopting the Nietzschean vision of the transvaluation of self. It was Nietzsche who finally understood that the only way to accept the world's meaninglessness was to shift attention to the self-as-historical-process and to transvalue successively what a man is at any given moment or stage of his life. The new century offers the phenomenon of such artists as Gertrude Stein, Joyce, Picasso, and Stravinsky constantly exploring, experimenting with, and finally mastering new styles, only to abandon them and go on to further exploration and experimentation. This constant transvaluation of the self and of the ways of symbolizing the self through style enables many twentieth-century artists to accept and thus resolve the paradoxes of existence. For Morse Peckham the "Bell Song" of Nietzsche's Zarathustra is the model for this mode of transvaluation and acceptance. By making the self the stage for self-violation rather than external violation, the new vision makes possible the continuity of self-renewal as well.

Nietzsche realized that this is neither a world which once held value nor a world which holds value now or a world which ever will hold it. It is without value, without order, without meaning. The world is nothing. Value and identity are the ultimate illusions. We emerge from nothingness and encounter the nothingness of the world, and in so doing, we create being. But being can be renewed only if we recognize that being is illusion. With that recognition as our ultimate weapon we can re-create it, not from sorrow but from joy. From the desire for value we create ourselves, but to renew that value, we must destroy ourselves. The profoundest satisfaction of the human mind is the creation of the world —

out of nothingness. From that act of creation emerges the sense of value, the sense of identity, which are sources of joy only if we recognize them as illusions. The sense of order, the sense of meaning, and the sense of identity are but instruments for the act of creation. Thus the Romantic once more enters into history and human life, for to create is to choose, without ever knowing whether or not the choice is the right choice, for the act of choice changes the world.[1]

Nietzsche finally makes manifest the tendency toward which all Romantic thought was leading. He shows, first of all, that the quest for value is misguided because it is only through the individual that value is projected onto the world. Indeed, the very concept of the quest is itself an illusion, just as is the need to find meaning. And so, by using the transvaluation of the self to transcend the quest for value, the Nietzschean Romantic opens the possibilities for the freedom of twentieth-century art, the freedom so supremely exploited by the great modernist novelists and poets, such as Joyce, Yeats, Eliot, and Faulkner — but a freedom comprehensible only in terms of the tradition out of which it grew.

Because of cultural lag, American literature seems at the end of the nineteenth century to break before the evolution of the Romantic dialectic into the major works of the Stylist orientation, whereas in European literature Stylism had developed alongside Naturalism two or three decades earlier. This book therefore ends with the novel that takes the Realist-Naturalist tradition as far as it is to go in American literature, *Sister Carrie*. But like all endings, this one is arbitrary, since the Romantic tradition continues in the twentieth century. Henry James breaks through into Stylism in his late phase, in a novel such as *The Ambassadors*, which is both a culmination of the nineteenth century as well as a beginning of the twentieth, since it explores many possibilities of the Stylist mode and also shows — although to a somewhat lesser degree than do the works of Joyce or Picasso — the artist's ability to transvalue the self by transvaluing an old style of symbolizing the self. The real possibilities of this new mode of vision are explored by those writers who finally begin to fragment the forms of their works to present as much as possible a self-created vision of the

1. Morse Peckham, "The Dilemma of a Century: The Four Stages of Romanticism," in *Romanticism: The Culture of the Nineteenth Century* (New York: Braziller, 1965), p. 33. This essay also appears in *The Triumph of Romanticism* (Columbia: University of South Carolina Press, 1970).

world. The struggle against human contingency expressed in the fragmented Symbolist visions of early modernist art is the major cultural drama of the new century, arising directly out of the Romantic dialectic of which it is the next genuine phase. It is therefore incumbent on everyone to understand the development of nineteenth-century Romantic culture in order to understand the origins of the present age.

INDEX